Becoming Your Best Possible Self

A Transformative Personal Growth Strategy Using the Power of Beliefs, Values and Attitudes

Gerard Morgan

Orla Kelly Publishing,
27 Kilbrody,
Mount Oval,
Rochestown,
Cork.
Ireland

CONTENTS

Overview vii

About the Author.. viii

Introduction 1

Chapter 1: A Model for Action...................................... 15

1.1 A Model for Action 16

1.2 Components of the Model 17

1.3 Situation 1 18

1.4 Situation 2 20

1.5 Key Take Aways 22

Chapter 2: Components of the Model - Beliefs............................ 24

2.1 What are Beliefs...26

2.2 Common Limiting Beliefs..27

2.3 Overcoming Limiting Beliefs.......................................32

2.4. Empowering Beliefs 34

2.5 Try This..45

2.6 Key Take Aways 46

Chapter 3: Components of the Model - Values............................ 48

3.1 What are Values 49

3.2 How to Discover our Values 50

3.3 Life Purpose 56

3.4 Try This..60

3.5 Key Take Aways 61

Chapter 4: Components of the Model -Mindsets and Attitudes ... 62

4.1 Mindset and Attitude...63

4.2 Importance of Attitude 65

4.3 Key Attitudes..67

4.4 Key Take Aways 69

Chapter 5: Examining Your Key Attitudes to Self **70**

5.1 Attitude to Self-talk 71
5.2 Attitude to the Present 87
5.3 Attitude to Goals 101
5.4 Attitude to Gratitude...115
5.5 Attitude to Creativity 120
5.6 Attitude to Action..125
5.7 Attitude to Habits 130
5.8 Key Take Aways 136

Chapter 6: Examining Your Key Attitudes to Situations............ **138**

6.1 Attitude to Failure and Difficulty 140
6.2 Attitude to Opportunity 150
6.3 Attitude to Change 154
6.4 Attitude to Productivity...158
6.5 Attitude to Communication...162
6.6 Attitude to Fear..170
6.7 Attitude to Learning...175
6.8 Key Take Aways 179

Chapter 7: Examining Your Key Attitudes to Others **181**

7.1 Attitude to Service/Contribution 182
7.2 Attitude to Negotiations 188
7.3 Attitude to Money 192
7.4 Attitude to Letting Go/Forgiveness.....................................195
7.5 Attitude to Relationships...201
7.6 Attitude to Seeking Help 208
7.7 Key Take Aways 213

Chapter 8: Becoming Your Best Possible Self **214**

Key Take Away...221
Conclusion 225
Bibliography...231

Appendix 1: How to Meditate 235
Appenxix 2: Best Possible Self Exercise 239
Index 245
Please Review 251
Bonus Items 252
About the Samaritans 253

Dedicated to my wife Mary and our sons Oisín and Daragh

100% of the profits from the sale of this book will be donated to Samaritans Ireland, registered charity 20033668.

OVERVIEW

The answer to Life's questions lay inside all of us. The book outlines the essential beliefs, values, mindsets and attitudes that are key to happy, successful, fulfilling, productive and purposeful living in a modern context. The book plots the journey from the Old Self to the Best Possible Self based on the new evidenced-based science of Positive Psychology and experts in their fields. In particular it is a journey from the external self to the internal self where the real power for human flourishing can emerge.

A simplified model is presented of how our Mindset and its component parts consisting of beliefs, values and attitudes is used for all our actions. Each of these components is explored in detail so that we understand their influence on behaviour. Key Beliefs, Values and Attitudes are examined which are often not taught in schools or at home. Knowing this information can greatly enhance everyone's approach to life.

The book is unique in that it uses many diagrams, pictures, relevant quotations and illustrations to clarify the points being made. Practical examples for implementing the knowledge in our daily lives are frequently offered. Another unique aspect of the book is that 100% of the profits from the sale of this book will be donated to Samaritans Ireland, registered charity 20033668.

A clear view of becoming your Best Possible Self emerges as a continuous process of self-discovery, self-improvement, self-acceptance and personal growth. From setting value-based goals and working to achieve them. From being true to yourself, serving others and having the right set of beliefs and attitudes –and becoming your Best Possible Self in the process.

About the Author

Teaching, learning and service has been a consistent theme in his life over the past 40 years. He was a business teacher for 3 years in a variety of secondary schools in Dublin. He moved from there to teach computers to Post Leaving Certificate students in Dublin. He published two computing books. From there he went into management roles of Deputy Principal and Principal of two Further Education Colleges for 20 years. He also lectured Higher Diploma in Education students in Maynooth University. For several years he was also the CEO of a Vocational Education Committee (VEC) now an Education and Training Board (ETB) and was responsible for many schools and Education centres.

He also has over 40 years experience in the voluntary sector volunteering for a scouting organisation, a national mental health charity and other community groups. He held senior leadership roles in these organisations for many years. He is now happily retired.

He has a passion for Personal Development and the growing evidenced-based science of Positive Psychology and its application for the betterment of all.

His career in education and personal development over the past 40 years has given him a unique insight into the development needs of people.

A graduate of Business, Computing and Education from University College Dublin and DIT, B.Comm, H.Dip Ed., Dip.O.Ed., AMBCS, M.Ed (specializing in Educational Psychology). He also completed an Advanced Diploma in Executive and Personal Coaching with Distinction.

INTRODUCTION

*"The answers to Life's questions lie inside you.
All you need to do is look, listen and trust."*
Cherie Carter-Scott

"Who looks outsides, dreams, who looks inside, awakens."
Carl Jung

"It is not the mountain we conquer, but ourselves."
Sir Edmund Hillary

"How are you going to win if you are not right within."
Lauryn Hill Doo Wop (That Thing) song

*"When you truly study top performers in any field, what sets them apart
is not their physical skill, it is how they control their mind"*
Dr. Stan Beecham

*"Until you make the unconscious conscious, it will direct
your life and you will call it fate."*
Carl Jung

*"Let today be the day you give up who you've been
for who you can become."*
Hal Elrod

*"Authentic happiness derives from raising the bar for yourself,
not comparing yourself to others."*
Dr Mark Seligman

"The source of all abundance is not outside you. It is part of who you are."
Eckhart Tolle

"Life is a process and it is never done."
Jadine Woodside

I remember well my days in primary and secondary school. There were always those students where everything came natural to them. They learned to read and write with ease. There was the rest of us where we had to work hard to understand and learn in school. I learned early on that attitude, motivation, and learning techniques and perseverance were just as important as innate ability.

In 5th year in secondary school, I remember getting to sit a test on study skills and motivation. I remember scoring the highest in the class. I had been just moved to a higher stream class following good Junior Certificate results. This was mainly due to extra tuition my father Charlie gave me that year. He instilled in me a love of learning which has stood to me to this day. I was particularly inspired by all his different learning techniques. In particular I liked memory techniques and structured study techniques. Things needed to be compartmentalised and visualised to be remembered and understood. I remember in particular the use of mind maps and mnemonics for learning concepts. At a young age I sought books out on these topics.

Teaching, learning and service has been a consistent theme in my life over the past 40 years. I was a business teacher for 3 years in a variety of secondary schools in Dublin. I moved from there to teaching computers to Post Leaving Certificate students in Dublin. I also published two computing books. From there I went into management roles of Deputy Principal and Principal of two Further Education Colleges for 20 years. I also lectured Higher Diploma in Education students in Maynooth University. For several years I was also the CEO of an Education and Training Board in Waterford responsible for many schools and Education centres. In addition to my professional life I have over 40 years experience in the voluntary sector volunteering for a scouting organisation, a national mental health charity and other community groups. I held senior leadership roles in these organisations for many years. I am now happily retired.

I often reflect on this time in Education and in the community and wonder has enough time been given to motivation, learning skills, wellness and life skills in general. Whilst studying for a Master Degree in Education I specialised in Educational Psychology which sparked my interested in the role of wellness and life skills teaching in general and in education. I also obtained a Diploma in Executive and Life Coaching and I have coached many people over the years which has given me the qualifications and experience to have a good understanding of human potential.

Often education consists of just a mass of facts and things to be learned and not enough understanding and life skills. Oscar Wilde is quoted as saying:

"Education is not the filling of a pale or bucket but the lighting of a fire."

This to me is the core of education, once the learner is inspired, interested and motivated, the learner themselves will want to learn and will learn. I had first-hand knowledge of this when my father gave me extra specific tuition before my Junior Certificate. Initially it was hard work every Saturday morning. However, at this time I was acutely aware that my father was giving me his time and I was sure he had many other pressing issues he could have been doing given I came from a family of seven children. His teaching approach was very patient and kind and if you did not understand he would try to explain it in another way. He used many memory techniques and made the whole process fun by introducing challenges, games and diagrams. He would always say the most important thing was my interest in and

3

attitude to learning. He often said to me if I wanted to learn that was *"half the battle"*. Eventually I found he lit the fire for me to learn and I became a self-motivated learner with the right attitude to learning.

My mother, Rena, is and was a great influence in my life also. She is a constant rock to all our family, she has amazing emotional intelligence and can sense how you are at a glance and is never shy to ask how you are really feeling. She is always supportive of us and supported us to pursue our own interests. She was very tactile and always gave us a hug in the morning or when it was needed. She was always good at giving subtle advice when it was needed. I remember her advising me to consider updating my computer skills at night part-time when I was a newly trained teacher in a particular college. I followed her subtle advice and I subsequently became Principal of that College. Sound advice indeed!

This got me thinking about the importance of attitude in life as well as learning. It also prompted me to think about what important lessons should be passed on to all students in school and to my own sons about essential attitudes for this great journey called Life. My own experience in school was that some of the essential attitudes and lessons for life were not taught. I believe they should have been taught to all at different stages in education. Far too often education is purely subject based where facts and knowledge are considered the most important. Whereas key concepts of creativity, resilience, key essential attitudes, beliefs, values are ignored. This prompted me to write this book and in particular to pass the wisdom and lessons in this book on to my two sons as a legacy. In doing so I hope this wisdom will help them to become their Best Possible Selves.

Another motivation for writing this book is my aspiration that the lessons and advice in this book will serve as many people as possible and have a positive impact on many lives. I hope, you the reader, find this book to be transformative and it helps you on your own journey to becoming your Best Possible Self. This ambition aligns with my own

Life Purpose of service and contribution. My motivation in writing this book is not financial instead my motivation is to have the maximum impact on as many people as possible through implementing and understanding the advice presented. For this reason I am contributing all the profits generated from the sales of this book to Samaritans Ireland. This charity provided essential 24/7 emotional support in almost a half a million interactions with those in need in Ireland in 2021 and is having a major impact on people's lives.

In writing this book I am seeking to document what I feel and what the experts are saying are the essential philosophies and tools for moving toward successful learning, living and happiness and ultimately becoming our Best Possible Self. I will begin with exploring a definition of success and happiness. From there we will look at essential concepts such as mindset, beliefs, values and key attitudes involved in following a new approach to fulfilment, happiness and success.

Ireland went through a long recession and equally before that a long boom called the Celtic Tiger in the 1990s. During this boom period many people in Ireland had accumulated unprecedented wealth. This created many very wealthy people in Ireland. Ironically, however, at the same time there was an increase in unhappiness and psychological problems. This begs the question if increased wealth correlates to increased happiness. In his controversial book "Affluenza" author Oliver James (2007) outlines the idea that the more affluent a society becomes the more likely its people will be affected by the affluent virus.

This contagious virus can cause depression, anxiety and addiction. This has been demonstrated by Oliver James across many different countries. The symptoms include wanting to be wealthier, famous, fashionable, consistently making comparisons with others. Possessions can be more important than people, shopping greatly occupies one's time, extrinsic values at work are very important, they seek luxury, status equals possessions and life is better the more you own.

In summary people affected by the affluenza virus are more focused on material, extrinsic, external things to give them happiness. This can lead to issues down the line and may not give the long-lasting happiness yearned for. As Robert Holden (2011) puts it in his book "Happiness Now" the EGO principle is at play. The EGO principle, he states, stands for Everything Good Outside, a very common Mindset in affluent societies. It is always chasing the world for success, happiness love and appreciation from external sources (outside). The problem with this approach is, the more you get, the more you want. There is no end to the wants. The assumption is, there is something missing inside and it must be looked for outside of one self. Holden and James contend that this is a big mistake.

Holden outlines in his book three routes to happiness

1. Doing where the key outcome is achievement.
2. Having where the key outcome is accumulating.
3. Being where the key outcome is acceptance.

Most people strive all their lives on doing and having. Holden argues that to be truly happy one must Be first and then one can do and have. The EGO approach focuses exclusively on doing and having. Holden argues that unless you are happy with yourself you will not be happy. His formula is:

True happiness = Self-acceptance (freedom from self-judgement)

Holden's focus is on the self or inside first and not the external. Holden states

"Happiness and self-acceptance go hand in hand. In fact, your level of self-acceptance determines your level of happiness. The more self-acceptance you have, the more happiness you'll allow yourself to accept, receive and enjoy. In other words, you enjoy as much happiness as you believe you're worthy of."

The *"Action for Happiness"* movement says that Acceptance (being comfortable with who you are) contributes considerably to happiness and is one of the movement's 10 keys to Happiness. This has been empirically proven by many major studies which can be access from this movement's website.

https://www.actionforhappiness.org/10-keys-to-happier-living/be-comfortable-with-who-you-are/details

The movement Action for Happiness is a movement for a happier society and was formed in 2011 and its Patron is the Dalai Lama. This movements pledge is "to create more happiness and less unhappiness in the world". This movement promotes happier living for all using some components of this new approach. I will refer to this Movement's advice where and when appropriate.

Another Author Ben Renshaw (2010) in his book "Successful but Something Missing" expands on this theme. He argues that true success is a state of mind (internal) and not achievement and possessions (external). He argues that there are two distinct approaches to success.

Approach one is the old approach of doing and having and keep wanting more. This is an outside approach where we search for success outside of ourselves. Our self-esteem is linked with our achievements and possessions. We are constantly comparing ourselves with others. We often compete on a win/lose basis. We struggle and strive to get success but it is never enough.

This old approach still dominates. It focuses on externals, it encourages us to aim for personal success, good grades, a good job, monetary success.

The new approach is an inner state of mind. Our self-esteem is based on our mindset and attitude and not our achievement. We open up the mind to the non-physical reality of the world. Success is being true to ourselves and our values. True nobility is not being better than somebody else but being better than you yourself used to be. It is all about growing as a person.

As Will Smith put it in his autobiography - "Will" as he is approaching 50.

"I had a bias toward action, thrusting, pushing, striving, struggling, doing – and I began to realise that their opposite were equally as powerful – inaction, receptiveness, acceptance, non-resistance, being.."

The Waterford doctor Dr Mark Rowe (2015) in his book "A Prescription for Happiness" explains this new approach thus:

"What's most important is not who you were, or even are right now, but who you are becoming along this journey called life." pg 257

In the "Alchemist" the author, Paulo Coelho (2020), tells us that the true treasure is where you are, but you need to go out and experience the world to know that. The real treasure he contends is who you have become as a result of looking for it. We become the Alchemist of our lives by turning lead to gold by becoming better than we used to be.

With this new approach, success is motivated by giving and opening to others. Success is often based on win/win thinking. Success encourages ease, relaxation and non-attachment. Success is enough using this approach.

Jim Rohn explains in his book "Keys to Success" that success is something you attract by the person you become, by your own personal development and what you become is much more important that what you do or have. He says:

"Success is the continual unfolding of the design of your own life."

This new second approach for me is the best to adopt in my opinion. From this concept I have considered a new approach which moves away from the EGO Everything Good Outside approach to what I call a EGI Everything Good Inside approach initially.

EGI infers an Inner approach. In order to explore this concept further I am keen to describe the Mindset and attitudes of this new approach. This approach assumes that everything we want and everything we are is already inside us. It is a journey without distance to a place we should have never left. The only mistake we make is to think that we are separate from the perfection when we were created.

"Hell on earth is to meet the man you could have been." Tony Robbins

It is very important to have a clear vision of who you want to BE. You need to write down the ideal person you want to be. And be crystal clear WHY you want to become this Best Possible Self.

We will explore this internal approach throughout this book.

This exploration will consider this new approach by looking at the concepts of mindset, beliefs, values and key attitudes for success and happiness. These are based on scientific evidence, studies and my own personal experience and these are referenced where appropriate.

The transition from the External approach (Old Self) to the Internal (Being) approach (Best Possible Self) is summarised in Table 1 and is the basis of the theme of this book.

Table 1: The Transition from Old Self to Best Possible Self

Old Self	⟶	Best Possible Self
Conditional acceptance of self	⟶	Unconditional acceptance of self
Doing /Having	⟶	Being/Doing/Having
Living	⟶	Living/Enlightenment/ Awakening
External Focus	⟶	Internal Focus
Everything good outside	⟶	Everything good inside initially
Learned Self	⟶	Original Self
Mind Full	⟶	Mindfulness
Am I Whole?	⟶	I am Whole/Self-Acceptance
False Self	⟶	Real Self
Lower level of Consciousness	⟶	Higher level of Consciousness
Fearful self	⟶	Loving self
Critical self	⟶	Non-Critical/ Affirmative Self
EGO	⟶	Soul /Spirit
Searching for Wholeness	⟶	Experiences Wholeness
Body/Mind	⟶	Body/Mind/Soul/Spirit
Dreams	⟶	Dreams/Awakens
Auto Pilot	⟶	Fully Conscious/Aware/ Mindful
Analysing	⟶	Sensing
Avoidance of Difficult Emotions	⟶	Approaching difficult emotions
Depleting Energy	⟶	Nourishing

Not living by Values	⟶	Living by Values
Unexamined Attitudes	⟶	Examined Attitudes
Unexamined Beliefs	⟶	Examined Beliefs
Unappreciative	⟶	Gratitude
Comparing with Others	⟶	Self-Acceptance/Personal Growth/Comparing with past Self
Striving	⟶	Accepting/Ease
Attachment	⟶	Non attachment
Uncreative self	⟶	Creative Self
Reactive self	⟶	Non-reactive/ Proactive self
Taking	⟶	Giving
I am not good enough	⟶	I am good enough
Powerless	⟶	Powerful/Responsible/ Proactive
No Goals	⟶	Goals Set in line with values and beliefs
Fixed Mindset	⟶	Growth Mindset
Adversity	⟶	Growth
Change	⟶	Opportunity
Thinking/Emotions	⟶	Awareness/Consciousness/ Being
Win/ Lose	⟶	Win/Win
Past and Future Focus	⟶	Present Focus
Unexamined Daily Habits	⟶	Examined and Empowering Daily Habits
Success is a destination	⟶	Success is the quality of the moments of the journey
Success is never enough	⟶	Success is enough

The transition from Old Self to Best Possible Self will be explained throughout the book and the elements of the table above will be explained in detail. I will refer to this table again at the conclusion where upon the reader will be crystal clear on what basis and more importantly how the transition can take place through practical examples and advice.

In the words of Benjamin Franklin:

"An investment in knowledge pays the best interest."

For the first time since the early 1990's the whole area of Positive Psychology is now giving us a chance to re-evaluate our lives based on empirical evidence. Positive psychology is the scientific field devoted to human flourishing. It focuses on the psychological notions of happiness, flourishing and well-being and focuses on making human life better. This in contrast to the traditional psychological approach which focuses in the main on the negative aspects of human psychology such as mood disorders or emotional shortcomings.

Martin Seligman, who founded the field of Positive Psychology defines it thus:

'[Positive psychology is] the scientific study of optimal human functioning [that] aims to discover and promote the factors that allow individuals and communities to thrive'.

Using the growing evidence and research being generated from the growing field of Positive Psychology from the past 30 years it is now becoming possible to map out new perspectives on happiness, success and flourishing and being in a modern context.

I hope that you the reader will benefit from the knowledge and examples in this book to allow you to learn key life lessons, mindsets, values and attitudes to allow you to become your Best Possible Self and lead a fulfilling life.

This is a continuous process of self-improvement, self-acceptance and growth. I would encourage you to follow the practical exercises and examples presented in this book in the many "examples" and "try this" sections to reinforce your learning and understanding and help you on your own personal growth journey.

I would like you to become personally involved with the material and advice in this book by experimenting with the examples and exercises given in the book. To fully understand this material you need to be fully engaged personally. As the old Chinese proverb says:

"Tell me and I will forget, show me and I may remember,
involve me and I will understand."

Becoming your Best Possible Self involves a continuous process of self-discovery, self-improvement, self-acceptance and personal growth. It is a journey, not a destination, in personal growth and contribution which we will follow throughout this book.

Key Take Aways

- The old approach to happiness/success/fulfilment is externally focused i.e., the emphasis is on doing (achievements) and having (possessions).

- The new approach to happiness/success/fulfilment is focused on being your Best Possible Self and is internally focused i.e., looking inside ourselves with the primary focus on Being and then having and doing.

- The key outcome of Being is Self-Acceptance.

- New evidence-based positive psychology is now giving us empirical evidence and direction for becoming our Best Possible Self-leading to greater fulfilment and happiness.

- A direction of Travel Table, (Table 1) is presented which maps out the transition from Old Self to Best Possible Self.

- Becoming your Best Possible Self involves a continuous process of self-discovery, self-improvement and personal growth. It is a journey, not a destination, in personal growth and contribution.

CHAPTER 1

A MODEL FOR ACTION

"What, then, makes a person free from hindrance and self-determining? For wealth doesn't, neither does high-office, state or kingdom—rather, something else must be found... in the case of living, it is the knowledge of how to live."
Epictetus

Introduction

We take actions/decisions all the time in our daily lives. But do we ever stop to think what influences these decisions and whether they are moving us in the right direction.

When we are considering the transition to the Best Possible Self it is important to analyse the influences/filters on our decision-making. Often our actions come about unconsciously i.e., without being aware of our influences/filters at play.

In this chapter we identify the key influences/filters as our beliefs, values, attitudes and mindset and these are important to our decision-making and ultimately our actions. It is imperative that we should examine these in some detail and this will be done throughout the book.

In this chapter we will explore:

- A very simple model of how we take decisions is presented and identifies the influences/filters at play.

- Two different situations are described to illustrate how the Model for Action works and the key influences.

- The Key Takeaways from the Chapter are identified for clarification.

1.1 A Model for Action

As stated in the introduction I was interested from a young age on the influence of attitude on our learning and life. This interest was initially sparked off when I was learning from my father. What I found from my research is that mindset, beliefs, values and attitudes are key components to how we live our lives and make decisions.

According to Stanford psychologist Dr. Carol Dweck, in her book "Mindset," your beliefs play a pivotal role in what you want and whether you achieve it. Dweck has found that it is your mindset that plays a significant role in determining our behaviour, achievement and success.

Your mindset is a set of beliefs that shape how you make sense of the world and yourself. It influences how you think, feel, and behave in any given situation. Mindset is an overarching concept which incorporate many of our individual attitudes, values and beliefs as a collective.

Diagrammatically we could represent how we take Action/ Decisions using our mindset as follows see Figure 1.1. This has 8 key components:

1. Situation
2. Mindset
3. Attitude
4. Beliefs
5. Values
6. Thought
7. Feeling
8. Your Action / Behaviour

1.2 Components of the Model

It is important to understand the component filters and processes used in our mind before we take Action.

In Figure 1.1 the diagram shows how we generally take action. Firstly, there is some stimulus or situation or question presented to us that we need to take action on. This is then taken in to our mind and it goes through 3 key filters. These are Our Beliefs, our Values and our Attitudes and are illustrated in the Mindset filter below. This process is very quick some research shows it happening in as little as 0.25 of a second.

Figure 1.1 A Model of how we take Action/Decisions

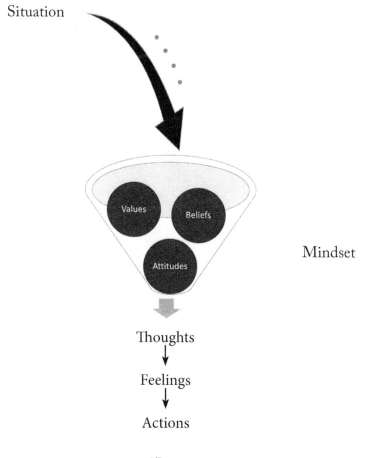

1.3 Situation 1

It is important that we look at these key components in more detail which is the basis of the next few chapters. However, we will look at one situation to illustrate how the model works but has two very different outcomes based on different filters used. A situation is given below in words with the five key components described. The mindset is pessimistic and the attitude is negative. These filters negatively affect the actions and feelings as a result.

Situation/Stimulus

- It rains on your holidays

Mindset

- Pessimistic (glass half empty)/Fixed Mindset

Attitude

- Negative self-talk

Beliefs (relevant)

- Holidays should be enjoyed at all times

Value (relevant)

- Free Time is important
- (Gap of 0.25 sec between stimulus and thought)

Thoughts

- This always happens to me
- This will ruin my holiday
- I paid good money to be in the sunshine and not the rain

Feeling

- Anger/Frustration

Action/Behaviour

- Go to the bar and drown my sorrows
- Give out to others

This situation can be illustrated diagrammatically in Figure 1.2 Model for Action below.

Figure 1.2 Situation 1 Model for Action

Situation
It rains on your sun
holidays

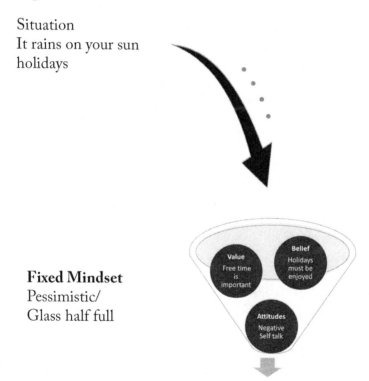

Fixed Mindset
Pessimistic/
Glass half full

Thoughts: This is not fair, this will ruin my holiday
Feelings: Anger and frustration
Action: Go to the bar and drown my sorrows, give out

1.4 Situation 2

The same situation is given below but with two different filters, the attitude and mindset, resulting in very different Actions from Figure 1.2. This could be described in words as follows and diagrammatically in Figure 1.3 below. The mindset is optimistic and the attitude is positive. These filters positively affect the actions and feelings as a result.

Situation/stimulus

- Rain on holiday

Mindset (different from Diagram 1.2)

- Optimistic (glass half full)/Growth Mindset

Attitude (different from Diagram 1.2)

- Positive self-talk

Beliefs (relevant)

- Holidays should be enjoyed at all times

Value (relevant)

- Free Time is important

(Gap of 0.25 sec between stimulus and thought)

Thoughts (different from Diagram 1.2)

- This is unfortunate but I will enjoy my holiday
- I will bring an umbrella
- There is no such thing as bad weather but inappropriate clothing
- I will do indoor activities until it stops
- This will pass
- I will learn from this

Feeling (different from Diagram 1.2)

- This is not so bad
- I can learn to deal with this

Action (different from Diagram 1.2)

- Enjoy the holiday despite the weather
- Wear appropriate clothing

Figure 1.3 Situation 2 Model for Action with different filters (Mindset and Attitude)

Situation 2
It rains on your sun
holidays

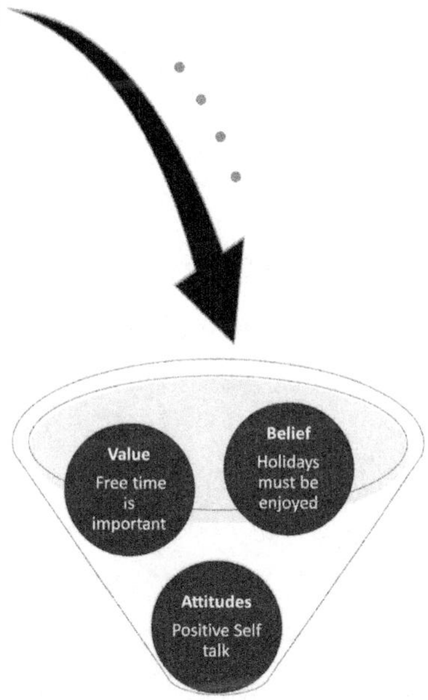

Growth Mindset
Optimistic/Glass
half full

Value
Free time
is
important

Belief
Holidays
must be
enjoyed

Attitudes
Positive Self
talk

Thoughts: This will pass, I will do indoor activities
Feelings: Ok as this will pass
Action: Enjoy holiday despite the weather, wear
appropriae clothing

This model is a simplification of how we make decisions and take action. The gap between the stimulus/situation and the final action/behaviour can be very small. Some researchers say the gap is as quick as .25 seconds. The average reaction time for humans is 0.25 seconds to a visual stimulus, 0.17 for an audio stimulus, and 0.15 seconds for a touch stimulus based on specific neuroscience experiments. For more details see https://backyardbrains.com › experiments › reactiontim

This gap is of major importance and is a source of our growth and happiness.

"Between stimulus and response there is a space. In that space is our power to choose our response. In our response lies our growth and our freedom."

Viktor E. Frankl, a neurologist, psychologist and Holocaust survivor

1.5 Key Take Aways

- A model for how we take action is presented which has 3 key stages, 1. A stimulus is presented of information, or a question or some situation that needs your decision and action, 2. The stimulus is processed in the mind using your mindset which is composed of our beliefs, our values and attitudes. 3. The result of this process is thoughts, feelings and action.

- The gap between the stimulus and response is very small and is our power which lies in this gap because we can choose how to respond. How we respond is based on our mindset which is composed of our beliefs, our values and attitudes.

- A deeper dive is needed to explore the key filters used to taking decisions/actions. The key influences/filters identified are:

- Our Mindset
- Our Beliefs
- Our Attitudes
- Our Values
- These influences/filters will be explored in detail in the remaining chapter of this book and their contribution to the transition to becoming our Best Possible Self will be considered.
- The Model for Action is represented diagrammatically again as follows:

Situation/Stimulus

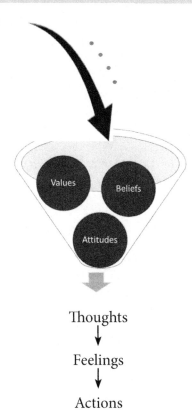

Thoughts

↓

Feelings

↓

Actions

CHAPTER 2

COMPONENTS OF THE MODEL -BELIEFS

"Man often becomes what he believes himself to be. If I keep on saying to myself that I cannot do a certain thing, it is possible that I may end by really becoming incapable of doing it. On the contrary, if I shall have the belief that I can do it, I shall surely acquire the capacity to do it, even if I may not have it at the beginning."
Mahatma Gandhi

"If you are distressed by anything external, the pain is not due to the thing itself but to your own estimate of it; and this you have the power to revoke at any moment."
Marcus Aurelius

"Your chances of success in any undertaking can always be measured by your belief in yourself."
Robert Collier

"What we can or cannot do, what we consider possible or impossible, is rarely a function of our true capability. It is more likely a function of our beliefs about who we are."
Anthony Robbins

"Believing in yourself trumps all."
Unknown

Introduction

One of the key filters we us in the Model for Action discussed in the last chapter is our Beliefs. It is important to take a deeper look at this key filter to understand how it can influence our behaviour. The elephant-and-the-rope story illustrates the power of beliefs.

When an elephant was a baby, a trainer ties a small rope around its leg and attaches it to a peg to keep it from running off. The elephant repeatedly attempts but fails to free itself due to its being small. Once the elephant is grown up, it can easily break the rope and gain the freedom of movement but it doesn't try. By then, the elephant has internalized the deep belief that the rope is stronger.

I think a lot of us are like that elephant. We are limited by old beliefs that do not accurately reflect our present capability. Until these beliefs are revisited, they will continue to reinforce the limitations on which they were based. It takes courage to try where we've failed in the past.

We need to recognise the limiting beliefs we have and challenge them and switch to more empowering and limitless beliefs based on our own soul aligned intuition, passions and inspirations.

When our beliefs are a reflection of our true nature, instead of limiting beliefs, we can shine our positivity wherever we go.

In this chapter we will explore in detail

- What are Beliefs
- Common Limiting Beliefs
- Overcoming Limiting Beliefs
- Empowering Beliefs
- Try This
- Key Take Aways

25

2.1 What are Beliefs

Beliefs are ideas you hold to be true.

They are often developed from our parents, our education, our culture, our faith, our societal conditioning and experience. They do not necessarily need to be true for us to believe in them.

These beliefs can control our behaviour. For example, our faith will have rules and if we believe in them, we will try to adhere to these rules.

Beliefs can be very strong as we know from the Placebo effect. Placebo is a believed positive effect. There are many well documented cases where patients are given a placebo drug, a dummy, but are not told this. They are told they have been given a drug and informed of its effects and because they believe it to be true, they actually experience the effects solely because they believed.

The Nocebo effect is the opposite. Nocebo is a believed negative effect. Again, many Harvard studies showed people developing negative physical and mental symptoms despite a dummy drug being administered. This is illustrative of the power of belief.

The key point here is if you believe something will have a negative effect it most likely will, or if you believe something will have a positive effect it will also. How many times do we listen to others giving us negative feedback or our own feedback and it affects us negatively?

Some beliefs can be empowering and others can be limiting.

Beliefs can determine the course of our lives. Beliefs determine how we think, interpret, act, and feel. Beliefs are based on how we make sense of our experiences and our perspective. Outdated beliefs may not be relevant today.

2.2 Common limiting beliefs include:

2.2.1. Common Limiting Belief -Your EGO is defining you

The EGO simply put is what you think of yourself.

EGO represents that part of ourselves that identifies with our self-image, personality, talents, accomplishments and perceived weaknesses, and possessions. The ego separates you from others. The ego makes judgments and longs to feel special.

This ego identity can be positive, based on your experiences and beliefs. If it is positive it will lead to high self-esteem and self-love. This can lead to high self-confidence.

However, the ego identity often is negative and loves conflict, creates enemies and operates out of fear. You begin to recognize yourself as your past, your social status or the shape of your body. The size of your bank account has a bearing on your EGO's identity. The difficulty with identifying yourself based on these external things is that they can be lost at any time and hence your ego is defining you and your identity could be lost. This is often referred to the false self or learned self as it differs from our original self when we were born in our natural state of perfection.

With the EGO defining you based on having and doing, you can see yourself as a conditional self. If you see yourself conditionally, you believe you must earn the right to be worthy. Your value and worth are conditional upon meeting certain criteria. You strive to achieve things to prove your worth to yourself and others by constantly doing and achieving. This is a very common belief and can be very limiting because at any time these external criteria can be lost and hence our identity can be lost.

2.2.2 Common Limiting Belief - I'm not good enough

"The belief in not being good enough is your ego's greatest addiction."
Holden Rebert

This is a very common inner belief to have according to Louise Hay in her book "You Can Heal Your Life" 2004

"The innermost belief for everyone I have worked with is always" I'm not good enough!"

Other versions of this include *"I am not worthy enough"* or *"I don't deserve this"* or *"I am unloved"* or *"I am unlovable."*

When you have this inner belief (which is often unconscious), you'll find that you can often be your own worst enemy.

You don't pursue your dreams because you don't feel you're good enough.

It also effects financial issues for example you might not apply for jobs with a higher salary because you feel you're not worthy.

Gerry Hussey (2021) explains in his Book "Awaken the Power Within" he had a belief that his father did not love him. He states that

"We experience the world not as it actually is but through the lens of our inner beliefs and expectations."

He gives the example of his relationship with his father which he interpreted using his own belief system. He gives examples of working with his father where his father was annoyed or tired doing a certain task with him and he would interpret this as his father being annoyed with him. When the author lost at sport, he would think his father was disappointed in him rather than disappointed for him. This was a case of his inner belief system working against himself and was confirmed (as he thought) incorrectly at every turn. As it turns out later the author was able to examine his relationship with his father and see that he was creating and confirming that he was not loved where in fact he was.

Hussey says

"I realised that my enemy, my demon, was nothing outside of me – it was not my dad, …my demon was my thoughts about myself, my inability to know and accept my real self."

Hussey advocates examining your limiting inner beliefs and to examine them closely to see if they were or are correct. Often these limiting beliefs are formed in childhood and carry on into adult life.

Hussey says

"The moment, when I began to see myself as someone that deserved love and respect, was the moment everything changed."

2.2.3 Common Limiting Belief - The world is not a safe place

Einstein is quoted as saying to a reporter

"The most important question that any person can ask is whether or not the universe is a friendly place?"

"What do you mean?" answered the reporter, *"How can that be the most important question?"*

Einstein responded solemnly

"The answer we find determines what we do with our lives. If the universe is a friendly place, we will spend our time building bridges. Otherwise, people use all their time to build walls. We decide."

What a life lesson, indeed!

Certain fears can be caused from the belief that the world is not safe. We might not want to take on challenges or change if we believe it might not be safe to do so. This can be a very limiting belief. The reality is that in the main the world is a very safe to be in. The media often highlights the bad news and this can colour this negative belief.

2.2.4. Common Limiting Belief - I am powerless

This could be the feeling of powerlessness to change, feeling that you have no power over your life circumstances or over what happens to you.

If you have this belief that you can't change anyway, then you're not likely to take the steps that are proven to work and give you the changes that you want.

Having the belief that I am powerless also means that you don't take responsibility for yourself. Instead, you blame other people or other situations for the way your life is at the moment. Jim Rohn tells a story in his book "The Keys to Success" (2013) when he gives a list of excuses to his mentor for not being successful. He blames the government, taxes, prices, his company, etc. He has a long list which he gives to his mentor. His mentor looks at the list and spends time to read it thoroughly. He then says to Jim that it is an impressive list but there is something missing from the list and that is YOU. YOU need to take responsibility for the life YOU have. YOU are the catalyst for change. It is not what happens it is what you do is the most important." The major key to your better future is YOU"

2.2.5. Common Limiting Belief - I need the approval of others to be happy

"To place the responsibility for your happiness on anybody other than yourself is a recipe for misery."
Will Smith

Every person must wage a solitary internal war for their own contentment. It is only natural that we seek the approval of others. We start this process early in life when we were children where we seek the constant approval of our parents. Disapproval is avoided at all cost. This process continues into adulthood but can become a problem in itself.

If we continuously need others approval, we are seeking approval of ourself from outside. This can be a problem as you can avoid doing things that are important to you but you will not do them because of the disapproval of others or society.

2.2.6 Other Limiting Beliefs

"I don't have enough resources": Believing that you don't have enough resources, such as money, time, or connections.

"I am not smart enough": Believing that you are not smart enough can prevent you from pursuing career or education opportunities that you may be qualified for.

"I am not worthy of success": Believing that you are not worthy of success can prevent you from and trying new things and taking risks.

"I am too old/young": Believing that your age is a limiting factor can prevent you from pursuing opportunities that may be available to you regardless of your age.

"I am not lucky": Believing that luck is the key to success can prevent you from taking action to achieving your goals.

2.3 Overcoming Limiting Beliefs

As Marcus Aurelius, philosopher, states:

"You have power over your mind; not outside events. Realize this, and you will find strength."

Here's a very simple activity based on Jack Canfield's "Success Principles" book (2015:286-287) activity that aims to help you overcome any limiting belief.

1. Identify a limiting belief or beliefs that is/are holding you back.

2. Write down a list of all the beliefs that are limiting, get a friend, a partner another family member to help and write down all the beliefs that your parents, guardians, friends, religion, teacher etc. that you hear that may be limiting you.

3. Go through your list and choose one that you think is still limiting you.

4. Determine how this belief limits you.

5. Decide how you would rather act or feel.

6. Then create a turnaround statement. Which should be called out daily to sink in.

   The limiting belief *"I am not good enough"* could be changed that to "I am good enough" or *"I am worthy enough"* or *"I do deserve this."*

   The limiting belief *"The world is a not a safe place for me"* could be changed to *"I live in a safe world in the main."*

   The Limiting belief *"I am powerless"* could be changed to *"I am powerful and can influence my world and I take responsibility for my actions."*

If you notice any resistance when saying these turnaround statements, you could try to modify these statements to replace the word "am" with the word "want" or "can" e.g., *I want to be good enough*" or "*I can be good enoug*h" etc.

7. We should try and focus on what we control as often we cannot change our circumstances.

"Focusing exclusively on what is in our power magnifies and enhances our power."
Ryan Holiday

This is what we can control and is in our power
*   Our thoughts
*   Our perspectives
*   Our attitude
*   Our creativity
*   Our emotions
*   Our effort
*   Our determination
*   How we spend our time

8. Focus on Empowering Beliefs

2.4. Empowering Beliefs

2.4.1. Empowering Belief - I accept myself unconditionally

If you have Unconditional Self Acceptance, your self-image and value is not conditional on meeting some external criteria relating to doing or having. You value yourself based on being true to yourself and your values and empowering attitudes.

You shift away from the EGO-defined self to a being which looks internally and away from thinking and emotions and toward a better version of oneself and a heightened sense of awareness and consciousness.

According to therapist Russell Grieger (2013), unconditional self-acceptance is understanding that you are separate from your actions and your qualities and possessions. You accept that you have made mistakes and that you have flaws, but you do not let them define you.

According to author Dr. Harry Barry in his book "Emotional Resilience" unconditional self-acceptance *"is the most important of all"* and is required for inner peace and Emotional Resilience. He calls it *"the real secret of good mental health"*.

The *"Action for Happiness"* movement says that Acceptance (being comfortable with who you are) contributes considerably to happiness and is one of the movement's 10 keys to Happiness. This has been empirically proven by many major studies which can be access from this movement's website. https://www.actionforhappiness.org/10-keys-to-happier-living/be-comfortable-with-who-you-are/details.

2.4.2 Empowering Belief - Strive to live at the highest level of Consciousness

When you shift away from thinking and emotions to Awareness and Consciousness (which is the power within the present moment) and Being (which is formless) a greater intelligence emerges free of the ego.

A psychiatrist, David R. Hawkins, M.D., PhD., after treating thousands of patients, began to see common levels of thinking, feeling and acting. He realized that people's challenges and advances were closely correlated to their level of consciousness. He published a scale measuring level of consciousness or vibration, in his bestselling book "Power Versus Force" (1995).

Hawkins and other researchers over three decades used kinesiology to measure the level of consciousness. He drew up a chart of consciousness levels in a scale from 1 to 1,000 (see chart below).

Map of Cosciousness Levels

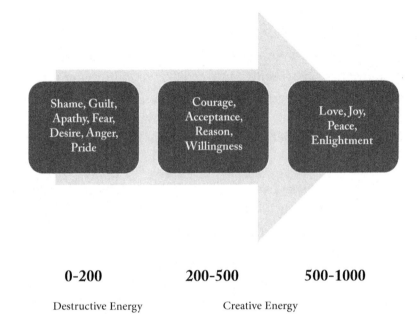

| 0-200 | 200-500 | 500-1000 |

Destructive Energy   Creative Energy

On the scale 200 is the level above which we begin to add energy to everything around us. Below 200 we are net consumers of energy.

Dr Hawkins' goal in creating the Map of Consciousness was to assist human evolution.

He explains the superiority of Power over Force:

"Force is experienced through the senses; power can be recognized only through inner awareness…. The only way to enhance one's power in the world is by increasing one's integrity, understanding, and capacity for compassion."

The Best Possible Self may be considered to be an evolving self moving along the increasing intensity of consciousness. Hawkins chart might give some idea of the transition. At the bottom, the focus is on negative emotions and external forces and these forces are destructive. In the middle when the focus turns to the internal and self-acceptance, the real power of being begins to appear. Beyond this there is great individual happiness, success and creativity.

Nearer the top of consciousness, one begins to emerge from oneself and become a person who has a positive influence on many people and ultimately on all of mankind.

2.4.3 Empowering Belief - Follow the path to my True Self

The notion of True Self is an idea of an essential, authentic aspect of a person's identity.

The idea of a "true self" is often associated with the notion of self-awareness, self-knowledge, and self-acceptance. It suggests that individuals who have a strong sense of their true self are more likely to experience a sense of coherence, purpose, and fulfilment in their lives.

Caroline McHughes states in her famous Ted talk "The Art of Being Yourself" February 2013 with over 12 million views to date. Caroline says:

"….you're not your thoughts because you think them. And you can't be your feelings, because otherwise who's the you that feels them? You're not what you have; you're not what you do; you're not even who you love, or who loves you.

There has to be something underneath all that, and when you look at people who have managed to transcend all these judgements that we put upon them" such as …"

— Barrack Obama ….., he couldn't be judged as a man, or a black man, or young, or old, or Democrat, or Republican, nor a gay, or a straight. It really wouldn't have mattered, because he knew why he was here. "Yes, we can."

Caroline continues to explain the Art of being your true self. She states that our true self is more evident when we are young, under 5, when we have no real sense of self. When you are young, you're fantastic at being yourself because you don't know how to disguise your differentness.

The other place you're fantastic at being yourself is when you're older, because you are more honest and less self-conscious. You become more honest and authentic.

McHughes says that there are 3 states of being. Superiority Complex, Inferiority Complex and finally the Interiority Complex.

The most important view of you is of yourself. However, if you have too positive a view of yourself, it can be a superiority complex or too poor view of yourself it can become an inferiority complex. According to McHughes, the best thing to do is to have a more balanced view of yourself which is in between these two extremes. This balance can be achieved by practicing humility which she defines as "Humility is not thinking less of yourself; humility is thinking about yourself less."

Your only job while you're here on the planet is to be as good at being you as they (people who know their true self) are at being them.

True self is often referred to as the Soul. The soul is not your mind or your thoughts but something at a higher level. It is accessed through your feelings of passion, intuition and inspiration. These feelings are not mind generated but come from a much deeper place. The mind and EGO as we know often come from a place of fear and over thinking whereas passions, intuition and inspirations emerge as signs for us in pure form.

Your Soul gives us access to these insights to be our true self. You do not choose you passions.

An example of somebody finding his true self is that of Dean Karnazis. When he was young he liked to run and ran in many races and was a successful runner in school. But when he was a teenager he lost interest in running as he developed other interests. He subsequently went to college and finished a business degree and MBA. He went on to have a good job in business.

One day he was celebrating his 30th birthday after work with his colleagues and it suddenly dawned on him that he did not like his job and he was miserable. He left the party early and instead of continuing to drink in the venue he decided to celebrate by running 50km instead. He felt elated that night when he completed the 50km run and knew from that moment he had to dedicate his life to running which he calls finding his best self.

What he did is the subject of his TED talk "Finding Your Best Self" which describes his many remarkable running feats such as completing 50 consecutive marathons in 50 days in 50 states in America, and he completed many ultra marathons of over 216km including runs in Death Valley and the first marathon to the South Pole. He also completed the Spartatalon a 246km race. His ultimate achievement was running 560kms in 80 hours and 44 minutes without sleep in 2005.

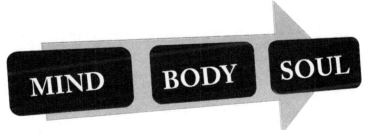

Figure: We are more than just "Mind and Body". We are "Mind and Body and Soul"

The multi-billionaire and author of "Principles" (2017) and business tycoon Ray Dalio says that we should spend time exploring our true self or our true nature. Having found this true nature he advises that we should follow this path towards and using our true nature for true success.

Dalio is in his seventies and he has offered to the world a free assessment which you can evaluate your true nature. He uses this assessment for his own employees in his company Bridgewater Associates.

The test takes 30/40 minutes and can be very revealing. The assessment is currently free to use and is available on the principlesyou. com site. It gives a full breakdown and explanation of your personality match and Archetype and how the results can play out in real life.

I found this assessment tool to be very accurate and revealing for my own exploration of my true self.

Another way to find your True Self is to ask yourself some of the following questions:

- What are my core values? What is most important to me in life? (see chapter 3)

- What are my passions and interests? What brings me joy and fulfilment? (see Chapter 3)

- What are my strengths and weaknesses? What do I excel at, and where can I improve?

- What are my fears and insecurities? What holds me back from being my true self? (see Chapter 6 section 6.6)

- What kind of person do I want to be? What kind of life do I want to create for myself? (see Chapter 3 section 3.3)

Achieving a connection with one's true self requires self-awareness, self-exploration, and self-acceptance.

2.4.4 Empowering Belief - I am Good Enough

"What I am is I am good enough, if I would only be it openly."
Carl Rodgers

You believe that you are good enough and deserve to be loved and respected as you are.

It is good to have a positive belief about yourself and to believe that you are good enough. Believing in yourself and your abilities can help you to achieve your goals and overcome challenges.

It is important to maintain a balance when believing you are good enough. It is good to have confidence in yourself but it is also important to acknowledge your weaknesses and areas where you can improve. This can help you to grow and develop as a person.

Everyone has strengths and weaknesses, and no one is perfect. We should not compare ourselves to others but focus on our own progress and growth.

2.4.5 Empowering Belief - The world is a safe place in the main

The reality is that the world is in the main a safe place to live in. Many parts of the world are relatively safe and individuals can take steps to minimise risks and ensure their safety. There are many exceptions to this where there is political unrest, war, extreme poverty and natural disasters.

2.4.6 Empowering Belief - I am in Control

I take full responsibility for my life by being proactive and making things happen for me.

Some things are out of my control but we focus on the things we can control to improve our lives.

Steven Covey in his book "7 Habits of Highly Effective People" says that the first habit of highly successful people is to take the responsibility for their Actions. He says successful people recognise this Responsibility as Response Ability which is the ability to choose your response. They are Proactive and make things happen. The opposite to proactivity is being reactive. They do not blame their circumstances, and conditions for their actions. They are proactive and act and are not acted upon.

These people use their circle of influence to Act. That is, they act on the things that they can do something about. They try to increase their circle of influence. See the following diagram.

Circle of Concern / Circle of Influence

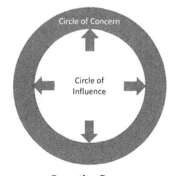

Proactive Focus

Positive energy enlarges the Circle of Influence

Reactive Focus

Negative energy reduces the Circle of Influence

© Steven R Covey "Circle of Concern / Circle of Influence

Being powerless often involves having a smaller circle of influence and a larger circle of concerns.

2.4.7 Empowering Belief - I do not need the approval of others to be happy

To change the habit of constantly seeking the approval of others you could try some of the following:

- Start by making decisions on what is right for you not based on approval from others. Self-knowledge is important to know what is right for you, so get to know your passions, what makes you feel good, your intuitions, your inspirations, and your values.

- Make decisions that are aligned to your true values, passions, intuition and inspirations.

- Try to reward and approve yourself so that you do not need the reward or approval from others.

- Practice Self Compassion. This is where you treat yourself as you would a good friend. You try to be less critical and more positive to yourself. If you can approve yourself and be compassionate more often this will become a more reliable source of approval and care as you have this source all the time. The approval from others can be variable and unreliable.

2.4.8 Empowering Beliefs - I Believe in the power of Empowering Attitudes to Self, Situations and Others

These include the believing in the key attitudes which are described in detail in the following chapters 5/6/7 as follows:

Key Attitudes to Self

- Attitude to Self-Talk
- Attitude to Present
- Attitude to Goals

- Attitude to Gratitude
- Attitude to Creativity
- Attitude to Action
- Attitude to Habits

Key Attitudes to Situations

- Attitude to Failure and Adversity
- Attitude to Opportunity
- Attitude to Change
- Attitudes to Productivity
- Attitude to Communication
- Attitude to Fear
- Attitude to Learning

Key Attitudes to Others

- Attitude to Service/Contribution
- Attitude to Negotiations
- Attitude to Money
- Attitude to Letting Go
- Attitude to Relationships
- Attitude to Seeking Help

2.5 Try This

- Identify as many limiting beliefs you have that you can think of. Write them down. You can use some of the common limiting beliefs identified in this chapter if you feel they are applicable to you.

- Write down a turnaround statements to counter each of the limiting beliefs you have identified.

- Identify as many empowering beliefs you have that you can think of. Write them down. You can use some of the empowering beliefs identified in this chapter if you feel they are applicable to you.

- Take the Free Assessment to find your True Nature/Self available at principlesyou.com website.

2.6 Key Take Aways Regarding Beliefs

- Beliefs are a key filter we use in our minds to make decisions and take action.

- Beliefs are very powerful whether they are true or not.

- Common limiting beliefs include:
  - Identifying ourselves with the ego
  - I am not good enough
  - The world is not safe
  - I am powerless
  - I need the approval of others

- Common limiting Beliefs can be overcome by:
  - Not identifying ourselves with the ego by practicing unconditional self-acceptance and being your true self aligned to your Soul through your passions, inspirations and intuitions.
  - Examine closely your belief that "I am not good enough" and counter this with the belief that you are someone who deserves love and respect.
  - The "The World is not safe" can be countered by looking at the facts in the world which is in general safe.
  - Powerlessness can be countered with what is under our control and within our circle of influence.
  - Needing the approval of others can be countered by self-compassion and aligning with your beliefs, values and attitudes.
  - The use of Turnaround statements is very effective to counter most limiting beliefs.

- Empowering beliefs can have a highly positive effect on our lives such as;
  - Accept myself unconditionally
  - Strive to live at the highest level of consciousness
  - Follow the path to my true self
  - I am good enough
  - The World is safe
  - I am in control
  - I do not need the approval of others
  - I Believe in the power of empowering Attitudes to Self, Situations and Others

CHAPTER 3

COMPONENTS OF THE MODEL - VALUES

"Open your arms to change but don't let go of your values."
Dalai Lama

"Keep your thoughts positive because your thoughts become your words. Keep your words positive because your words become your behaviour. Keep your behaviour positive because your behaviour becomes your habits. Keep your habits positive because your habits become your values. Keep your values positive because your values become your destiny."
Mahatma Gandhi

"If we want the deepest level of life fulfilment we can achieve it in one way, and that is by deciding upon what we value most in life, what our highest values are, and the committing to live by them every single day."
Tony Robbins

"When your values are clear to you, making decisions become easier."
Roy E Disney

Introduction

Life can be more satisfying when we know our values and when we make plans and decisions that align and honour our values.

If for example we value Family and have a job that requires us to travel and stay away from home often there might be an internal conflict there against the limited time we have with our family.

When you know your values, it can help when you are making key decisions such as what career to follow, what promotion is important, how should I spend my spare time, how I spend my money.

Values are usually stable but over time can change over the course of our lives. So, it is important to evaluate your values frequently.

In this Chapter we will look at the second component of the model for action Values. We will explore the following topics in detail.

- What are Values?
- How to Discover our Values.
- How we use our Values to help define our Life Purpose
- Try This
- Key takeaways from the Chapter

3.1 What are Values

Values are things that are important to you in the way you live and work.

They should determine your priorities and tell you if your life is turning out the way you want it to.

When what you do matches your values you can be satisfied and content. But when you do things that don't align with your values, that's when you can have a real source of unhappiness.

This is why making a conscious effort to identify your values is so important.

3.2 How to Discover our Values

In order to determine what our values are it is useful to follow the following steps:

1. Recognise the time/s when you were most HAPPY/ PROUD /SATISFIED/PASSIONATE/INSPIRED and ask yourself, what was I doing, why was I so happy/proud/satisfied/ passionate/inspired and what values were at play.

2. Think of some positive role models who inspire you. This can include people you know personally, famous people, characters in a movie or book etc. Consider what qualities and actions and values you admire about them.

3. Think of a time when you felt very strongly about an issue and took a particular stand and action on an issue. Why did you feel so strongly about the issue what values were at play? For example, Rosa Parks (1913—2005) helped initiate the civil rights movement in the United states when she refused to give up her seat to a white man on a Montgomery, Alabama bus in 1955. The United States Congress has honoured her as "the first lady of civil rights" and "the mother of the freedom movement". Rosa obviously felt so strongly about the apartheid system that she took this very dramatic and brave step. Her strong values of Fairness and Equality were at play.

4. List all values from steps 1-3.

5. Identify more values from the list below and choose and write down every value that you think is important to you. As you read through the list, write down the words that are an important value to you personally. If you think of other values not listed below add them to the list. The list below is in alphabetic order.

Abundance, Acceptance, Accountability, Achievement,

Advancement, Adventure, Advocacy

Ambition, Appreciation, Attractiveness, Authenticity, Autonomy

Balance, Being the Best, Benevolence, Boldness, Brilliance

Calmness, Caring, Challenge, Charity, Cheerfulness, Community, Commitment, Challenge, Compassion, Cooperation, Collaboration, Consistency, Cleverness, Contribution, Creativity, Credibility, Curiosity

Daring, Decisiveness, Dedication, Diversity, Dependability

Ethics, Excellence, Expressiveness, Empathy, Encouragement, Enthusiasm, Environment

Fairness, Family, Friendship, Flexibility, Freedom, Fun

Generosity, Grace, Green, Growth, Giving

Flexibility

Happiness, Health, Helping Others, Honesty, Humility, Humour

Inclusiveness, Independence, Individuality, Innovation, Inspiration, Intelligence, Intuition

Joy

Kindness, Knowledge

Leadership, Learning, Love, Loyalty, Low Carbon,

Making a Difference, Mindfulness, Money, Motivation

Optimism, Open-Mindedness, Originality

Passion, Performance, Personal Development/Growth, Proactive, Professionalism, Peace, Perfection, Playfulness, Popularity, Power, Preparedness, Punctuality

Quality

Recognition, Risk Taking, Relationships, Reliability, Resilience, Resourcefulness, Responsibility, Respect, Responsiveness

Taking, Teamwork, Thankfulness, Thoughtfulness, Traditionalism, Trustworthiness

Safety, Security, Service, Spirituality, Stability, Security, Self-Control, Selflessness, Simplicity, Stability, Success

Understanding, Uniqueness, Usefulness

Versatility, Vision

Warmth, Wealth, Well-Being, Wisdom

Zeal

6. Group all similar values together from your list of values you created. Group them in a way that makes sense to you, personally. Create between five to eight groupings. If you have more than eight groupings, drop those least important. See a sample below of a list of values groupings that emerges from step 5 above.

Abundance Growth Wealth Security Freedom Independence Flexibility Peace

Acceptance Compassion Inclusiveness Intuition Kindness Love Making a Difference Open-Mindedness Trustworthiness Relationships

Balance Health Personal Development Spirituality Well-being

Cheerfulness Fun Happiness Humour Inspiration Joy Optimism Playfulness

Appreciation Encouragement Thankfulness Thoughtfulness Mindfulness

7. Choose one word within each grouping that best represents the label for the entire group. Again, do not overthink your labels. There are no right or wrong answers. You are defining the answer that is right for you. See the example below – the label chosen for the grouping is underlined.

Abundance Growth Wealth Security <u>Freedom</u> Independence Flexibility Peace

Acceptance Compassion Inclusiveness Intuition Kindness Love <u>Making a Difference</u> Open-Mindedness Trustworthiness Relationships

Balance Health Personal Development Spirituality <u>Well-being</u>

Cheerfulness Fun <u>Happiness</u> Humour Inspiration Joy Optimism Playfulness

Appreciation Encouragement Thankfulness Thoughtfulness <u>Mindfulness</u>

These are my personal groupings (I had 8 groupings)

Charity, <u>Caring</u>, Kindness, Service, Spirituality, Compassion, Empathy, Humility Love, Fairness

Loyalty, Resilience, reliability, Professionalism, Consistency, <u>Commitment</u>, Dedication, Punctuality

Personal Development, Leadership, Learning, <u>Growth</u>, Making a Difference, Proactive, Motivation, Creativity, Balance, Safety, Adventure, Challenge, Inspiration

Appreciation, <u>Acceptance</u>, Awareness, Abundance, Thankfulness

<u>Fun</u>, Humour, Enthusiasm, Happiness, Open minded, Optimism

Friendship, Love, <u>Family and Friendship</u>

<u>Wellbeing/Health,</u> Mindful, Aware, Attitude

<u>Environment</u>, Green, Low Carbon

8. Finally, Rank the Values identified, in step 7. above. This can be difficult to do but is worth the investment in time. This ranking should be reviewed regularly as they can change over time. In fact, Tony Robbins (2001) advocates changing on purpose the rank of values from time to time in order to achieve major change and shift in the quality of peoples' lives.

My Ranked Values currently are

1. Family and Friends
2. Wellbeing/Health
3. Growth
4. Caring
5. Acceptance
6. Fun/Happiness
7. Commitment
8. Environment

My Values

Part of the values exercise should be to map out what type of person you want to become based on your values. This is a critical part of the Values exercise because you need to align your values with the person you wish to be. This exercise is very commonly used by psychologist to increase optimism and has been proven to be a very beneficial exercise.

Based on my values exercise I created this set of aspirations to BE.

3.3 Life Purpose

"Your time is limited so don't waste it living someone else's life. Don't be trapped by dogma which is living with the results of other people's thinking. Don't let the noise of others' opinions drown out your own inner voice. And most importantly, have the courage to follow your heart and intuition. They somehow already know what you truly want to become."
Steve Jobs past CEO Apple Computers

"The challenge for our generation is creating a world where everyone has a sense of purpose. Purpose is that sense that we are part of something bigger than ourselves, that we are needed, that we have something better ahead to work for. Purpose is what creates true happiness."
Mark Zuckerberg CEO Facebook

"My soul is not contained within the limits of my body. My body is contained within the limitlessness of my soul."
Jim Carey

The Values Exercise above is often used to form the basis for the forming of a *"Life Purpose."*

Richard Leider the author of "The Power of Purpose" says that Life Purpose looks like a clear-eyed, energetic person getting up in the morning — with a reason to get up in the morning — and going off to do something that they have really chosen to do with their time and their life."

Leider gives a formula for setting your life purpose:

Life Purpose = Gifts + Passions + Values

- Gifts are your talents and not just what you are good at but what you love to do and come easy to you.

- Passions are the things you are passionate about and these give you power to engross yourself in them. If you enjoy what you're doing and it is fulfilling, you're going in the correct direction. If not, it's time to readjust your course. Pay attention to what you are most passionate about, what inspires you and what your intuition is saying to you. And most importantly bring your soul-inspired wants into reality through your ACTION.

Developed by Chris and Janet Attwood, The Passion Test is a simple process to generate what your passions are. You start by filling in the blank 15 times for the following statement: "When my life is ideal, I am ___." The word(s) you choose to fill in the blank must be a verb.

For me some of my statements looked like this:

- My life is ideal when I'm being of service to people.
- My life is ideal when I'm empowering people
- My life is ideal when I'm coaching/teaching to groups.
- My life is ideal when I'm being part of a happiness network.
- My life is ideal when I'm being part of something bigger than myself.........

These then need to be ranked and the first 5 ranked statements used to form part of your Life Purpose statement.

Values are, as already discussed, deep-seated notions which you believe are important to you. You could ask yourself "What can I do with my time that is important to me" to align my values with my purpose.

Combining gifts and passions and values and aligning them can help you create a life purpose. The starting point is to spend your time doing things you care about, and from that, find a larger sense of purpose in the world.

Purpose is always outside of yourself, and larger than yourself. The opposite of purpose is self-absorption. For example, Nelson Mandela was all about his people, his country, and the larger common good outside of himself.

Life Purpose does not have be a grand vision like that of Nelson Mandela but for most of us it is a balance between saving and savouring. And purpose is about that balance. Life Purpose can come from simple things, like a job or project, a book you want to write, a child you want to see grow, a person you want to be with or passion you want to pursue or promote.

According to Wayne Dyer author of "Your Erroneous Zones" nobody needs to ask the question what is my purpose. It will always be found in service. If you can put for one day your attention on making life better for someone else. Put your mind on how I can serve. Business can be seen as service also by viewing it as serving your customers.

According to Dwyer the Purpose Driven Life is centred around the 4 Cardinal Virtues

1. Reverence for all life
2. Sincerity/Honesty
3. Sense of Kindness
4. Service

The Ego always want to be right, own things and achieve. It is mind constructed and controlled.

The Soul on the other hand knows exactly how to fulfil its purpose by being true to the feeling of passions, intuitions and inspirations. It is not mind controlled but guided by the constant and true self and your inner compass which needs to be trusted.

My current Life Purpose is as follows

"My life is based on the question "how can I serve.?" I will serve by being self compassionate and using my core values of caring, commitment, growth, fun, family, health, happiness, environment and acceptance."
Gerard Morgan

Serving the needs of people re advice, listening, books, coaching, caring, financial, etc.

Other Life Purposes for your inspiration include:

"To be a teacher. And to be known for inspiring my students to be more than they thought they could be."
Oprah Winfrey

"I shall not fear anyone on Earth. I shall fear only God. I shall not bear ill will toward anyone. I shall not submit to injustice from anyone. I shall conquer untruth by truth. And in resisting untruth, I shall put up with all suffering."
Mahatma Ganda

"If something is important enough you should try, even if the probable outcome is failure."
Elon Musk

"To make people happy."
Walt Disney

Rick Warren book "The Purpose Driven Life" is a bestselling book which sold over 50 million copies. He says we have been given stewardship of affluence and influence; and we are responsible for what we have been given.

He asks all of us "What are you doing with what you have been given?" He says that the purpose of influence is to speak up for those who have less influence. If money made you happy then all rich people would be happy which is not the case.

3.4 Try This

1. Go through the Values Exercise in 3.2 and identify your own Ranked Top 8 Values. Put these in your diary, phone and on your noticeboard and mirror so that you can see them everyday.

2. Use these Values to help you Define your own Life Purpose. Draw up your Life Purpose by using the formulae below and the examples given in this chapter and elsewhere.

   Life Purpose = Gifts/Strengths +Passions + Values.

3. Use your ranked values to ensure they are available when you are setting important Goals (in section 5.3 in Chapter 5).

3.5 Key Take Aways regarding Values

- Values are the things that are most important to you in the way you live your life.

- We need to live our lives in alignment with our values in order to be happy and fulfilled.

- Hence the need to spend some time to identify our Values and this can be done using a method outlined in this Chapter.

- Values should be ranked and lived by daily.

- Values can be used to map what type of person you aspire to be.

- Values can help to form the basis of your Life Purpose.

- Very few people explore their values or know them however they are essential to you becoming your Best Positive Self.

CHAPTER 4

Components of the Model -Mindsets and Attitudes

"The only disability in life is a bad attitude."
Dale Carnegie

"The greatest discovery of all time is that a person can change his future by merely changing his attitude."
Marie Osmond

"Weakness of attitude becomes weakness of character."
Albert Einstein

"If we are growing we are always going to be out of our Comfort Zone."
John Maxwell

Introduction

A man sells helium balloons on a side street coloured red, blue and yellow. On a bad sales day he releases one of the balloons into the air to boost sales. When children see the balloon going up into the sky they usually want to buy one and do the same.

One day a boy asks the vendor if a black balloon was released would it too fly into the sky. The vendor replies to the boy's question with empathy saying that yes a black balloon would fly up into the sky. He explains that it is not the colour of the balloon that is important but what is inside is the most important – the Helium gas which is lighter than air.

The same concept applies to our lives. It is what is inside us that is most important and that is our attitude and it is this attitude inside that makes us succeed and be our Best Possible Self.

In this chapter we will consider

- The concept of Mindsets including Fixed and Growth Mindsets.
- The concept of what Attitudes are and why they are important.
- Identify Key Attitudes of Self, Situations and Others.

4.1 Mindset and Attitude

Mindset is how you see the world around you. It is an overarching concept which incorporate many of our individual attitudes, values and beliefs as a collective.

Attitude is how you interact with the world in specific situations according to how you see things. It is how you treat yourself, others and how you approach situations based on your values and beliefs.

Mindset can be seen as a set of attitudes, values and beliefs, some similar, some different.

We might say that we have an optimistic Mindset or outlook which might consist of many specific attitudes such as positive self-talk attitude, a positive attitude and beliefs to failure and change and a positive attitude to service and gratitude. We saw this in Chapter 1 in the Model for Action.

On the other hand, we might say that we have a pessimistic Mindset or outlook which consist of many specific attitudes such as a negative self-talk attitude, a negative attitude to failure and change, and a negative attitude to service and gratitude.

As a person we can have different attitudes towards different aspects of life. One might have an easygoing attitude on Personal life but an attitude of a perfectionist at Work. Thus, a collection of such attitudes becomes a 'Mindset'.

Mindset is something that serves you every minute of the day. But you have to make the choice to cultivate and apply a healthy, serving, purposeful mindset which is made up of many different attitudes, beliefs and values.

Dr Carol Dweck spent her entire career studying Mindset and attitudes and performance. She concludes that Mindset and Attitude is a greater predictor of your success than IQ.

Dr Dweck (2017) in her book "Mindset" says there are two Mindsets that exist in general.

The Fixed Mindset which is where you believe your aptitude and attitudes and who you are is fixed with fixed beliefs and intelligences and that will not change. When challenges are presented often this mindset can be limiting and cannot adapt. It will not be open to change.

The Growth Mindset which views your aptitude and attitudes are changeable and open to growth. It will improve with effort. It embraces change and will adapt to change and opportunity. Aversity is seen as an opportunity to learn or change.

Dweck states that it is important to note 3 things about Mindset

1. Recognise the concepts of Fixed and Growth Mindsets as official with empirical proof of its existence and influences.

2. Learn how to develop your abilities and expand them to get the most from a Growth Mindset. Getting out of your Comfort Zone is very important for the Growth Mindset.

3. Listen for your Fixed Mindset Voice. If you hear yourself saying "I can't do it" change it to "I can't do it YET."

   If you understand the Fixed and Growth mindsets, you will see how one thing leads to another— how a belief that your qualities are fixed leads to a host of thoughts and actions, and how a belief that your qualities can be cultivated leads to an abundance of different thoughts and actions.

4.2 Importance of Attitude

"A happy person is not a person in a set of circumstances but rather a person with a certain set of attitude."
Hugh Downes

"When you change the way you look at things, the things you look at change."
Wayne Dyer

"We are what we think, thinking make it so."
Henry Ford

"Happiness is a state of mind that you create by the way you process and interpret the events of your life (attitude)."
Monk sold his Ferrari

"The last of the human freedoms is to choose one's attitude in any given set of circumstances."
Victor Frankl survivor of a Nazi concentration camp.

The greatest discovery of my generation is that a human being can alter his life by altering his attitudes of mind."
William James

"Attitude is Everything."
Dr Wayne Dyer

The Oxford Dictionary definition of Attitude is "a settled way of thinking or feeling about something". These settled ways of thinking or thoughts need to be constructive in order to be effective. Attitude is the way you choose to see things. Attitudes are intentional and should not be confused with emotions which are often involuntary states.

Attitude is how you treat yourself, others and how you approach situations based on your values and beliefs.

65

Your attitudes make you successful or happy not your circumstances. If I can control my attitudes and resulting thoughts, I can therefore control my happiness.

There have been a number of studies conducted, and they all conclude pretty much the same thing; mental attitude accounts for about 85 percent of our success in life, while skills and knowledge make up the balance.

Other well know authors have demonstrated the importance of attitude to performance and success. The Master Programme by Brian Tracey (1993) in his book "Maximum Achievement" uses this formula:

Individual Human Performance = (Inborn Attributes +Acquired Attributes) * Attitude

This formula indicates that attitude is the most significant aspect of human performance. Inborn attributes are the things that we are naturally good at. Acquired attributes are the things we have been trained in or learned along the way. But without attitude these two attributes do not significantly boost performance.

In Maureen Gaffney's (2021) book "Flourishing" she states that research has shown that the major determinants of happiness are genetics 50%, life circumstances 10% and 40% intentional activities we choose to pursue including the way we choose to think (attitude) and behave.

Colin Turner in his book "Born to Succeed" states that attitude contributes to 90% of people's success.

90% attitude 10% other attributes.

If key attitudes (part of mindset) are so important to success I would like to take a closer look at some key attitudes listed in section 4.3.

4.3 Key Attitudes

There are many different key attitudes which I feel and many experts agree are essential to the transition to the Best Possible Self. I have divided them into 3 categories.

- Attitude to Self
- Attitude to Situations
- Attitudes to Others

Attitudes to Self

Attitude is how you treat yourself, others and how you approach situations based on your values and beliefs.

Attitudes to self are the attitudes in the definition above which refer to "how you treat yourself". These are attitudes which are personal to yourself and your internal approach to yourself. They are your internal guide to how you see yourself and how you organise yourself internally.

I will be describing these attitudes to self in detail in Chapter 5. They include the following:

- Attitude to Self-Talk
- Attitude to the Present
- Attitude to Goals
- Attitude to Gratitude
- Attitude to Creativity
- Attitude to Action
- Attitude to Habits

Attitude to Situations

Attitude is how you treat yourself, others and how you approach situations based on your values and beliefs

Attitudes to situations are the attitudes in the definition above which refer to "how you approach situations". These are attitudes in common key situations or circumstances and how you approach these circumstances which in my opinion and many experts opinion are the best attitude to have in each key situation.

I will be describing these attitudes to Situation in detail in Chapter 6. They include the following

- Attitude to Failure and Adversity
- Attitude to Opportunity
- Attitude to Change
- Attitude to Productivity
- Attitude to Communication
- Attitude to Fear
- Attitude to Learning

Attitude to Others

Attitude is how you treat yourself, others and how you approach situations based on your values and beliefs.

Attitudes to Others are the attitudes in the definition above which refer to "how you treat….others". This refers to key attitudes to how we treat others which in my opinion and many other experts opinions are the best attitude to have when dealing with other people and things.

I will be describing these Attitudes to Others in detail in Chapter 7. They include the following:

- Attitude to Service/Contribution
- Attitude to Negotiations
- Attitude to Money
- Attitude to Letting Go
- Attitude to Relationships
- Attitude to Seeking Help

4.4 Key Take Aways regarding Mindset and Attitudes

- Mindset is how we see the world and is composed of 3 key filters of Beliefs, Values and Attitudes.
- Mindset can be Fixed or Growth.
- A Growth Mindset is the best as it is changeable and open to growth.
- A happy person is not a person in a set of circumstances but with a certain set of attitudes.
- Attitudes are how you approach different situations, ourselves and how you treat others.
- Many books and studies have outlined the critical importance of key attitudes to success some studies showing it is responsible for over 80% of our success.
- Key attitudes to self, situations and others are listed. These will be explained in details in the next 3 chapters.

CHAPTER 5

Examining Your Key Attitudes to Self

Introduction

Attitude is how you treat yourself, others and how you approach situations based on your values and beliefs.

Attitudes to self are the attitudes in the definition above which refer to "how you treat yourself". These are attitudes which are personal to yourself and your internal approach to yourself. They are your internal guide to how you see yourself and how you organise yourself internally.

I will be describing the key Attitudes to Self in detail in this Chapter. They include the following:

- Attitude to Self-Talk
- Attitude to Present
- Attitude to Goals
- Attitude to Gratitude
- Attitude to Creativity
- Attitude to Action
- Attitude to Habits

Putting these key attitudes to self into practice will help you greatly on your own journey to becoming your Best Positive Self.

For each Attitude to Self, I will describe the following

- What is the Attitude

- Why it is Important
- What advice is given for this Attitude
- Examples of this Attitude in use
- Try This yourself

5.1 Attitude to Self-Talk

"What a liberation to realize that the "voice in my head"
is not who I am. Who am I then? The one who sees that.
The awareness that is prior to thought…"
Eckhart Tolle

5.1.1 What is Attitude to Self-Talk?

Attitude to Self Talk is the way you approach how you talk to yourself in your head. We all do it.

Self-talk is basically your inner voice, the voice in your mind that says the things you don't necessarily say out loud. We often don't realise that this running conversation is going on in the background, but our self-talk can have a big influence on how we feel about who we are. We can get in trouble when we get stuck in the way we self-talk.

There is two types of Self Talk:

- Positive Self Talk
- Negative Self Talk

Positive self-talk makes you feel good about yourself and the things that are going on in your life. It's like having an optimistic voice in your head that always looks on the bright side. This increases happy hormones. It is like having a hero in charge of your self-talk where you see the positive and are hopeful and look to the present and future.

Examples: 'I am doing the best I can', 'I can totally make it through this exam', 'I don't feel great right now, but things could be worse'

Many people have a constant thought I am not good enough and think negative thoughts. Self-criticism, guilt and fear cause more problems than anything else according to Louise Hay author of "You Can Heal Your Life" which sold more than 50 million copies.

Hay advocates that self-acceptance and approval in the now are the key to positive changes in all areas of our life. This begins with never criticising ourselves or anything. She advocates that turning this self-criticism on its head with affirmation in the present tense (positive self-talk) are the way forward. Such as I am, I have, I approve of myself, etc.

Negative self-talk makes us feel bad about ourselves and the things that are going on. It can put a negative spin on anything, even something good. It is like having a villain in charge of your self-talk and constantly sees the negative and is doubtful and looks to the past for failures and evidence. Research again shows that 80% of our thoughts are negative. That's a lot of negative thoughts (80% of 80,000 = 64000 per day) This increases stress hormones and can also affect you physically. Negative self-talk often involves recalling negative experience from the past and this then becomes a negative thought. For example, you had a difficulty making a speech in the past this may be recalled if you have to do another one.

Examples: 'I should be doing better', 'Everyone thinks I'm an idiot', 'Everything's is getting to me', 'Nothing's ever going to get better.'

Negative self-talk tends to make people miserable and can even impact on their recovery from mental health difficulties. But it's not possible, or helpful, to be positive all the time, either. So, how can you make your self-talk work for you?

"It is hard to fight the enemy who has outposts in your head."
Sally Hempton

Our primitive brains are wired in such a way to listen much more attentively to negative or danger signals purely as a survival skill. In primitive times man had to be careful to listen out for noises in the bush in order to avoid been eaten by possible predators. The consequences of not listening to something negative could mean life or death and was an essential basis for survival. The consequences of not paying attention to something positive often did not threaten survival but may mean missing an opportunity.

So, the bias of our attention is to the negative and it is stored in the long-term memory as important to remember. News media are very aware of this human bias and use negative news stories to sell more media.

"If we don't change our inner view of ourselves, then it doesn't matter what we change on the outside, we still face the same negative self-talk."
Gerry Hussey

A lot of the time negative thinking/self-talk can be automatic and we are not very conscious of it happening. These are often called Automatic Negative Thoughts or ANTs. There are many types of ANTs type thinking which I will describe in the examples given below.

5.1.2 Why Attitude to Self Talk is Important

The way you talk to yourself can impact your life and your success. The effect can be good or bad depending if your self-talk is positive or negative. Research has shown that we typically have between 50-80k thoughts per day. Thoughts can affect us both physically and mentally in a positive or negative way.

The more you work on improving your self-talk, the easier you'll find it. It's like practising an instrument or going to sports training: it won't be easy to start with, but you'll get better with time.

It might not seem like much, but self-talk is a huge part of our self-esteem and confidence. By working on replacing negative self-talk with more positive self-talk, you're more likely to feel in control of your life and to achieve your goals.

5.1.3. Advice for Attitude to Self Talk

- Self-talk is your inner voice, it can be negative or positive.

- Practice positive self-talk as it can be empowering and can be improved with the use of Affirmations (many examples are given below).

- Negative self-talk is very common and damaging and automatic these are called Automatic Negative Thoughts ANTs. Use ANTi -ANTS to challenge and improve your negative bias (19 different techniques are given).

- Recognise your own self-talk patterns and write them down and name them.

5.1.4. Examples of Attitude to Self Talk

Mirror Test Example of Positive Self Talk

Author Louise Hay gives an example of the Mirror test she gives to her clients. Most people have negative thoughts when they look in the mirror. Hay asks her clients to say and find something positive about themselves every time they look in the mirror. She advocates saying "I love and approve of myself exactly as I am."

The thoughts you choose to think create your experiences. You are in control of your thoughts and your mind. Your mind is not in control. You are the master of your mind.

Louise Hay Example of Positive Self /Affirmations

Louise uses this affirmation in her daily routine:

"Louise you are wonderful, and I love you.

This is one of the best days of my life

Everything is working out for your highest good

Whatever you need to know is revealed to you

Whatever you need comes to you

All is well."

In her book she lists a comprehensive list of affirmations for many ailments and situations which over 50 million readers have found useful.

Self-Love and self-acceptance must come from within yourself. It does not need validation from others to be validated. We need to be able to self-congratulate ourselves when we move closer to who we want to be and achieve our goals.

Wayne Dyer Example of Positive Self Talk

Wayne uses this affirmation quote below before going asleep as the subconscious mind controls most of our thoughts.

Dwyer advises in the last 5 minutes before going to bed to follow the following affirmation routine.

Realise you are about to programme your subconscious mind, which is most at home when you are sleeping.

Before going to bed if you review all the things that happened to you this day and what you did not like, you are programming your mind to focus on all the bad things, you are marinating in these thoughts instead he advises to be very careful how we programme the subconscious mind.

What you place into your subconscious mind in last minutes before sleep is important as these thoughts will stay there in your subconscious mind overnight. The affirmation that is repeated most often is the one that's going to be most effective.

Dwyer advocates saying this passage taken from the book "The 3 Magic Words"

"I know that I am pure spirit,
that I always have been, and that I always will be.

There is inside me a place of confidence and quietness and security where all things are known and understood.

This is the Universal Mind. of which I am a part and which responds to me as I ask of it."

Personal Example of Positive Self Talk Affirmations

Irish people find affirmations difficult as they feel it is boastful and brash. However, we should try to think like the Americans who have no issues with talking themselves up. It is purely just saying what you are.

Examples of a list of daily affirmation I use every day:
- I am alive
- I live in a mainly friendly universe
- I am a kind and fair person
- I am enough
- I am becoming a better person all the time
- It is OK to be not OK sometimes

- I love myself
- Every day is a new opportunity
- I am in control
- I have many good qualities.

Final example of Positive Self Talk Affirmations

In his book "Love Yourself Like Your Life Depends on It" by Kamal Ravikant, the author was miserable and there were days where he could not get out of bed as he was too depressed. One day he hit his "emotional threshold," and got out of bed and wrote himself the following affirmation which he uses regularly:

"This day, I vow to myself to love myself, to treat myself as someone I love truly and deeply—in my thoughts, my actions, the choices I make, the experiences I have, each moment I am conscious, I make the decision I LOVE MYSELF."

Examples of Automatic Negative Thoughts –ANTs

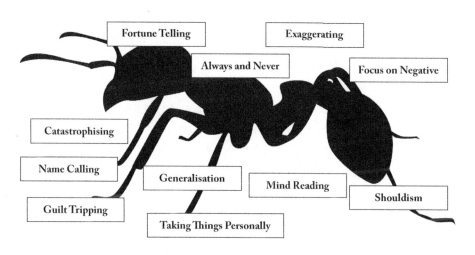

Always and never thinking this is where thinking is negative and absolute e.g.," I will never get a raise," "Nobody cares for me."

Focusing on the Negative thinking this is where we cannot see the positive in any situation only the negative, e.g. "That exam result was all down to luck."

Catastrophizing thinking this is where you are predicting the worst outcome, e.g., if I do not pass the exam, I will never get a job, Global warming will kill us all.

Generalisation this is where everything is generalised e.g. "I usually put my foot in it, that is typical of me."

Exaggerating this is where you are exaggerating the negative, e.g., "nobody likes me because I come from the city."

Mind Reading this is where you think you know what others are thinking, e.g., "she did not say hello to me this morning so she must be mad at me ". This is a dangerous practice as more often than not our mindreading is incorrect.

Taking things personally this is where you are blaming yourself for something that may not be your fault e.g., "they don't like me because they ignored me". We should not take things personally. People who say things usually are concerned with themselves e.g., they say you look great when they are feeling good themselves or they might say you are looking bad when they are feeling bad. Often the criticism or praise is more a reflection on the other person and not you. Negative Gossip can be toxic but is more a reflection on the person that is spreading it. This advice is one of the four key elements in the book "The Four Agreements" by Riouel Ruiz. We should remember the following quotes in relation to not taking things personally.

"Choose not to be harmed and you won't feel harmed. Don't feel harmed and you haven't been."
Marcus Aurelius

"Any person capable of angering you becomes your master; he can anger you only when you permit yourself to be disturbed by him."
Epictetus

<u>Name Calling</u> this is where you call yourself names e.g. "I am a fool, stupid."

<u>Shouldism</u> this is where you use should e.g. "I should meditate in the mornings, I should get up earlier."

<u>Fortune telling</u> this is where you predict the future which is often not based on any evidence e.g. "I am going to be awful at that presentation."

<u>Guilt trip thinking</u> this is where you focus on what makes you guilty or ashamed, e.g.," I am too shy to go to that party."

There are many more ANT type thinking and you should recognise these whenever you can.

Here are some ways to help change the direction of your self-talk based on well-researched data from many sources. We could call these ANTI-ANTs.

Examples of ANTI -ANTs

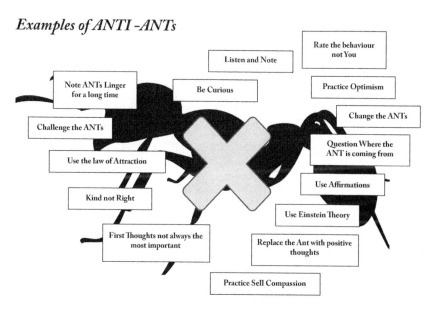

1. <u>Listen to what you're saying to yourself</u> and write it down

Notice what your inner voice is saying.

Is your self-talk mostly positive or negative?

Each day, make notes on what you're thinking. Negative self-talk can evoke strong emotions which are stronger than our logical mind. But by writing them down the logical mind can have a chance to evaluate them logically. Use of a journal to record your self-talk which allows you to review it.

2. <u>Get a name for it</u>

Recognise the different styles of thinking (see ANTs above) and write them down and name them in a notebook. Doing that we are observing the ANT in the moment this is hard to do, once we have a name for it this allows us to have more awareness in the moment and allows us to examine it. Skill acquisition for this recognition can be slow and takes a while. It is hard to catch negative self-talk in the moment, a day later is ok, if you can catch it in the moment this is the sweet spot.

3. <u>Rate your behaviour not yourself</u>

When you are being critical about something do not personalise it, focus on the behaviour instead. E.g. if your thinking was not productive in this case instead of saying to yourself "I am stupid" say to yourself "my thinking was less productive today I must learn from this, how could I do better next time."

4. <u>Try to be Optimistic (glass half full)</u>

As a general approach to self-talk, it is a good idea to take the approach of optimism. Realistic Optimism is even more real world as it knows there will be bad days where the optimism will be challenged but its approach is to try to see the good in a challenge and remind oneself that this will pass sometime.

5. <u>Challenge your self-talk.</u>

Ask yourself things like:

Is there actual evidence for what I'm thinking?

Can I do anything to change what I'm feeling bad about?

Is this thinking helpful to me at this very moment?

6. <u>Practice being kind and not right all the time</u>

Often people are constantly pushing and arguing to be right. Often there is negative self-talk present when you are trying to be right e.g., waiter is delayed with getting an order to the table but the restaurant is very busy. You would be right to be annoyed but you could replace being annoyed with the waiter with an acknowledgement that they are very busy and you understand.

7. <u>Change your self-talk</u>

Make a list of the positive things about yourself.

Instead of saying: 'I'll never be able to do this', try: 'Is there anything I can do that will help me do this?' You could say to yourself cancel this cancel this using the gap between stimulus and response as already discussed in Chapter 1.

8. <u>Start to be aware of triggers</u>

Be aware of triggers (certain people, situations, medical conditions etc.) so you can anticipate some of your negative thinking situations and triggers and catch it before it happens or at least be aware of the triggers and be prepared for the ANTs that follows.

9. Your first thought is not always the most important

This is worth thinking about as our thoughts often just flow but are in no particular order so we should be aware of the fact that the first thought that comes in to your mind is not always the most important one. So, the first ANT that comes to mind is not necessarily the most important it is just the first thought.

10. Replace an ANT with something else to divert your thinking

11. Self Compassion / Learning to treat yourself the same as somebody else or friend

When we are struggling our self-talk is intense and tough on ourself, we are so hard on ourselves.

However, if a friend came to you with the same problem we would normally not be as harsh on them with the same issue. Why is that? We should treat ourselves the same as we would treat others in the same situation. This can be transformative, give it a try for one week and see what happens. Ask yourself regularly this question:

What would I say if a friend were in a similar situation with the same negative thoughts as I have?

For further information on the huge benefits of self-compassion these are explored in-depth by Dr. Kristin Neff . She has been studying self-compassions' power over the past 10 years. She has many free resources and videos including her famous TEDx talk on this topic. See her website self-compassion.org for more information.

12. Be Curious

If you tend to be very harsh and judgemental in your thinking you could change this by being curious about your thinking. E.g., I am being very harsh on myself why is that ? Where did that come from?

This curiosity then diverts your negative thinking to curiosity rather than harshness.

Normally the first negative thing we hear or feel is usually early in our childhood from most likely a parent or a teacher. We internalise this and usually associate a powerful emotion with this and we try to avoid any potential situation again. This can make us fearful or negative. Often a common fear is that we are not good enough and this drives much human suffering. We need to deal with and examine these fears and ask are they serving us well.

13. Let Go

Wayne Dyer gives a good analogy of an Orange. When we squeeze an orange, we will only get orange juice and nothing else. So, when we are squeezed or upset often what comes out is what is inside. This can often be negative thoughts such as anger frustration bitterness etc.

He gives a further analogy of a snake bite. He states that you do not die of a snake bite but by the venom that remains for a long time in the body. The same is true of negative thoughts and emotions that are stored in our minds which we hold on to and have the same lingering affect as the venom. Dyer states that we should let go of these negative thoughts and emotions if we are to be free of them. This could involve forgiving and letting go.

Dyer expands on this by saying Nature's way of healing is to say close up a wound fast. If we get a cut our immune system tries as fast as possible to close up the wound by forming a scab.

However, the negative thoughts and issues of the past are often held on to and the wounds never heal. So, when we are squeezed and upset these naturally long-held unhealed wounds will come out. We need to let go of these negative thoughts in order to heal them if possible.

Stored and undealt with negative thoughts will resurface if they are not dealt with. This is referred to as the "Pain body" and become a trigger in the future. (see Chapter 7, Section 7.4 for a more detailed explanation of Letting Go)

14. <u>Replace an ANT with positive thoughts</u>

It is shown by research in Maureen Gaffney's book "Flourishing" that it can take 5 positive thoughts to cancel out one negative thought. We need enough credit for the inevitable stress and strains of life. So, we need to practice plenty of positive thoughts to negate the negative ones.

When is the last time you looked in the mirror and felt pride and love? What and who changed that ?. Try the next time to find positive things about yourself when you look at the mirror. Practice this often and see how it changes your negative self-talk.

15. <u>Replace something Missing in my Life with it is on its way</u>

If you are what you think about you need to be very careful what you think about. Be cautious with every conversation with yourself or others regarding what you are missing in your life. The law of attraction will attract more of what you are missing if this is a dominant thought. Your thoughts and emotions expand to what you are thinking.

Try not to talk about what is missing in your life change this to "ITS ON ITS WAY".

16. <u>Use Affirmations as an alternative to negative self-talk</u>

See the discussion on positive self-talk above and note this quote from Louise Hay:

"Remember, you have been criticising yourself for years and its hasn't worked. Try approving of yourself and see what happens."

17. **Practice Gratitude daily**

This is a technique used by many people which involves writing down daily at least 3 things you are grateful for every day. This can be difficult at first because of the fact that our mind has a negative bias. However, when we get into this practice the mind will start to actively seek out moments and events to be thankful for. This will counter the negative bias. It is best practice to record these gratitude lists in a Journal if possible.

Even on a day where everything goes wrong it is still possible to find some things that in your day you can be grateful for. (see Chapter 5, Section 5.4 for a more detailed discussion of Gratitude)

18. **Use the Law of Attraction**

The Law of Attraction is the idea that what we think comes to us or is attracted to us. So, if we are thinking negative thoughts, we will attract more negative things to us. If we expect bad things to happen to us, they are more likely to happen to us. Conversely if we expect or ask for more good things to happen, they are more likely to happen to us.

The process is explained as simple. It is a three-part process:

1. Ask for what we want (positive).

2. Believe in your heart and thoughts that you have it, really feel with your senses having received what you want.

3. The Universe will provide from here.

This is the power of positive thought. For example, if we express gratitude for the things we have we will attract more from this exercise.

Athletes are often coached to visualise a race going well for themselves in their heads. This can have very positive effects on the performance of the athlete in the actual race.

The book "The Secret" tells us that we should follow our bliss more and the things that make us happy and the law of attraction will attract more of this bliss to us.

19. <u>Do I live in a friendly or a hostile universe</u>

As discussed in the Beliefs section the answer determines what we do with our lives. If the universe is a friendly place, we will spend our time building bridges. Otherwise, people use all their time to build walls. We decide.

5.1.5 Try This

Practical ways to make your Attitude to Self-Talk work for you

- Recognise your own self talk patterns and write them down and name them. Are they positive or negative?

- Be aware of and use Positive Self Talk and Affirmations. Generate your own Affirmations and put them in your Diary and phone and read them out every day.

- Be aware of Negative Self talk and put them in your Diary and phone and read them out every day. Use some or all the 19 ANTi ANTs techniques to minimise their negative effects.

5.2 Attitude to the Present

"The ability to be in the present moment is a major component
of mental wellness."
Abraham Maslow

"Be happy in the moment, that's enough. Each moment is all we
need, not more."
Mother Teresa

"Children have neither a past nor a future. Thus, they enjoy the present,
which seldom happens to us."
Jean de La Bruyère

"Yesterday is history. Tomorrow is a mystery. Today is a gift. That is why it
is called the present."
Alice Morse Earle

"If you pay attention to the present, you can improve on it. And if you
improve on the present, what comes later will also be better. Forget about
the future, and live each day. Each day, in itself, brings with it an eternity."
Anthony Cehello

"Pay attention to the intricate patterns of your existence
that you take for granted."
Doug Dillon

"The ego's greatest enemy is the present moment…"
Eckhart Tolle

"The present moment is the field on which the game of life happens."
Eckhart Tolle

"Our very Presence becomes our identity, rather than our
thoughts and emotions."
Eckhart Tolle

5.2.1. What is Attitude to the Present?

Attitude to Present is your approach to the present moment in your Life.
The Oxford languages definition of Present is:
"The state or fact of existing, occurring or being present" (in the here and now).
The Journey is a passage that outlines the idea of the present-oriented Attitude or approach well, here is an extract:

"....Success is every minute you live. It's the process of living. It's stopping
for the moments of beauty, of pleasure, the moments of peace. Success is not
a destination that you reach. Success is the quality of the Journey."
Jennifer James

5.2.2 Why Attitude to the Present is important?

One of the most important pieces of information I have found in my research is that living in the present is the best place to be and will have a profoundly positive effect on your happiness. Why is this? It is because most negative thoughts /concerns are from the past and future thoughts. One of the most prolific writers on this topic is Eckhart Tolle. In his book "The Power of Now" he outlines in detail this concept. He remembers being very low in his life and even suicidal. But one morning he woke up with a new awareness of everything around him which awakened all his senses. The sunlight streaming through the curtains, the sound of the traffic on the street, the smell of the grass, the refreshing sensation of a simple glass of water, and the delicate brush of the breeze on his face. This awakened state stayed with him for many weeks and he was euphoric.

He reflected on this time of acute awareness and noticed it had a very positive effect on how he thought and felt. When he analysed this for himself, he noticed that he was very focused on the present moment and the feelings and stimulation of his senses.

His detailed analysis of this time made him curious about why this present focus was so beneficial. He noticed that thinking of the past tends to cause mainly difficult issues of the past to arise in the present and take over his mind and result in unhappiness. The mind wants these issues/thoughts as often they are seen by the mind as part of your identity. This was equally true of thinking of the future as most of future thoughts were about fears about the future most of which were false. As Mark Twain famously said:

"I have known a great number of troubles, but most of them never happened."

These past and future thoughts formed the basis of the constructed self in the mind. Jim Carey makes the point that what we fear in our minds and what actually happens are very different.

"There is a huge difference between a dog that is going to eat you in your mind and an actual dog that going to eat you!"
Jim Carey

According to Tolle many people identify with this constructed self in the mind. This is a major error as the constructed view of self in the mind is often incorrect and often works in an automatic or subconscious level. The subconscious mind is often very negative and consists of many very limiting and destructive self-beliefs. The mind is often over active the majority of which is negative.

He advocates we should become the observer of our thoughts and observe any future or past thoughts which are not in our best interest and switch to the present moment as much as possible.

He goes even further to say that we have a never changing "I" which is the observer of our thoughts which is the pure consciousness and true self. This true self is the source of our creativity and has been linked to our being, our conscious mind or free mind and our Soul.

In a later book "New Earth" the author Tolle expands on the idea of being and states that the most significant thing that can happen to a human being is the beginning of the separation process of thinking and awareness. This awareness takes over you're thinking and puts you in the present.

To access the present or NOW this can be done by Meditation, Mindfulness, the use of the observer of the mind. The author also stresses not to identify with your constructed mind. You are not your mind or the person you think you are.

The reason why people engage in dangerous adventurous activities such as rock-climbing, car racing etc. is because it forces them into the now which is the intensely alive state free of time. You cannot be thinking of the past or future worries when your next move on the rock face could mean life or death. For most of us we do not have to engage in these high-risk adventures to get the benefit of this NOW state. John Lennon put it in his own words "Life is the things that are happening when you are busy making plans for the future."

People are substantially less happy when they are mind wandering no matter what they are doing according to a major study carried out in the US called the Happiness Project. One finding was that 40% of those surveyed in the study were mind wandering most of the time and these mind wanderings were bad thoughts, regrets or worries in the future.

Another finding of this study was that when people are present in the moment then they are often happiest and the findings are represent in the bar chart.

Happiness Levels when Mind Wandering V Present Focused

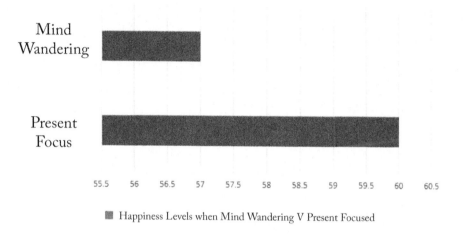

Happiness Levels when Mind Wandering V Present Focused

The advice from the researchers on the Happiness Project is to make sure you notice where your attention is, bring it back if the wandering is not productive.

Another book "Stumbling on Happiness" by Daniel Gilbert did its own study on happiness and according to their study of 2250 people it was found that just under half of the people are checked out or mind wandering. 46.9% people are shown to be generally not happy when they are mind wandering.

Dr Stan Beecham states is his book "Elite Minds" that top performers make it their business to understand and manage their unconscious wandering mind and master their conscious thoughts.

From "The Monk who sold his Ferrari" Robin Sharma 2000, he says that most of us miss out on life's big prizes, The Pulitzer, the

Nobel, Oscars, Toni's and Emmys but we are all are eligible for life's small pleasures in the present moment such as:

- A pat on the back
- A kiss on the cheek
- An empty car park space
- A crackling fire
- A glorious sunrise/sunset
- Hot soup on a cold day
- Cold beer on a hot day
- A mountain walk
- A child's smile
- A clear blue sky
- A word of praise
- A perfect ace in tennis
- The sound of rain on a tin roof

The advice is not to fret about getting life's grand awards but enjoy its tiny delights in the present and there is plenty for all of us. Make your own list and review and add to it regularly.

Happiness is found in the moments not year by year or month by month or day by day but by moment by moment. We all need to get the most of each moment and moments are special so we need to collect as many as possible. Living in the moment dispels regret and stress. Each day is a new beginning a new life full of moments to be cherished and savoured.

Finally in relation to the importance of living in the present Nadine Stair's (age 85) poem "If I Had My Life to Live Over" sums up her present approach to living:

".....Oh, I've had my moments and if I had it to do over

again, I'd have more of them. In fact,

I'd try to have nothing else. Just moments.

One after another, instead of living so many

years ahead of each day."

5.2.3 Advice for Attitude to the Present

- Try to live in the present moment as much as possible.

- Observe the mind and observe any future or past thoughts which are not in our best interest.

- Use as many methods of staying present as possible which include:

  - observing the mind

  - practicing meditation (see explanation in 5.2.4.1 and Appendix 1)

  - practice mindfulness (see explanation and examples in 5.2.4.2)

  - relish and saviour in the present

  - get in to flow states

  - consider life as a journey of moments.

- The advice is not to fret about getting life's grand awards but enjoy its tiny delights in the moment and there is plenty for all of us. Make your own list and review and add to it regularly.

5.2.4 Examples of Methods of Staying Present

5.2.4.1 Meditation

"My boss taught me to mediate which was to have a profound effect on my life and Career."
Deepak Chopra

"Quiet the mind and the Soul will speak."
Ma Jaya Sati Bhagavati

"Meditation is not about stopping thoughts, but recognizing that we are more than our thoughts and our feelings."
Arianna Huffington

What is meditation

"Mediation is focusing your mind on one thing."
Dermot Whelan

I like Whelan's reference in his book "Mind Full" to meditation as throwing cold water on our amygdala so that we are less reactive and sensitive. Our amygdala is our ancient part of our brain which operates to sense danger and is responsible for our flight or fight response to negative events whether true or imagined.

The Goal of mediation is to give the mind a mental break from the normal over-thinking state. It may be an ancient tradition, but it's still practiced in cultures all over the world to create a sense of calm and inner harmony.

Benefits of Meditation

There are many scientific studies which have shown the following benefits of meditation including the heighten sense of physical and psychological well being.

Refer to Davidson, RJ Kabat-Zinn,et al 2003 "Alterations in Brain and Immune Function produced by Mindfulness Meditation" Psychosomatic Medicine, 65 (4), 564 -70 and to Healthline.com/nutrition/12 benefits of meditation:

1. Reduce Stress and control anxiety

2. Promote emotional health

3. Enhance self-awareness

4. Strengthen attention span

5. Reduce age-related memory loss

6. Can generate Kindness

7. May fight addiction

8. Improve sleep

9. Help Control pain

10. Decrease blood pressure

There are nine popular types of meditation practice:

- **Mindfulness Meditation** Mindfulness meditation originates from Buddhist teachings and is the most popular meditation technique. You pay attention to your thoughts as they pass through your mind. You don't judge the thoughts or become involved with them. You simply observe and take note of any patterns.

- **Spiritual Meditation** It's similar to prayer in that you reflect on the silence around you and seek a deeper connection with your God or Universe.

- **Focused Meditation** Focused meditation involves concentration using any of the five senses. For example, you can focus on something internal, like your breath, or you can bring in external influences to help focus your attention.

- **Movement Meditation** It's an active form of meditation where the movement guides you. It can include yoga and also mediating and being mindful when walking or gardening etc.

- **Mantra Meditation** This type of meditation uses a repetitive sound to clear the mind. It can be a word, phrase, or sound, such as the popular "Om."

- **Transcendental Meditation** Transcendental Meditation (TM) is a technique for transcending (going above/avoiding) distracting thoughts and promoting a state of relaxed awareness. ... when meditating, the ordinary thinking process is "transcended." and replaced by a state of pure consciousness.

- **Progressive Relaxation** Also known as body scan meditation, progressive relaxation is a practice aimed at reducing tension in the body and promoting relaxation. This form of meditation involves slowly tightening and relaxing one muscle group at a time throughout the body.

- **Loving-Kindness Meditation** It typically involves opening the mind to receive love from others and then sending a series of well wishes to loved ones, friends, acquaintances, and all living beings.

- **Visualization Meditation** Visualization meditation is a technique focused on enhancing feelings of relaxation, peace, and calmness by visualizing positive scenes or images. With this practice, it's important to imagine the scene vividly and use all five senses to add as much detail as possible.

- **Guided Mediation** This is where you are guided through the mediation through an audio recording by a teacher. There are many of these available on the internet for free and others require payment. Some that I found useful are at www.headspace.ie.

How to Meditate

I have placed instructions on how to Meditate using 3 methods of meditation in Appendix 1 in this book and I give the example of the method I personally use.

5.2.4.2 Example of Using Mindfulness to be present

What is Mindfulness

Rob Nairn's definition of mindfulness is being the practice of 'knowing what is happening, while it is happening, no matter what its is.'

Jon Kabat Zinn's definition, "mindfulness means paying attention in a particular way: on purpose, in the present moment, and nonjudgmentally."

The "Action for Happiness" movement says that People who are Living Mindfully are happier and is one of the movement's 10 keys to Happiness. This has been empirically proven by many major studies which can be access from this movement's website. https://www.actionforhappiness.org/10-keys-to-happier-living/live-life-mindfully/details.

Personal Example of Mindfulness

I recently took up sea swimming on a daily basis. The question comes to mind "how do you know if somebody is a sea swimmer?" Answer "they will tell you so". I do not want to be that person but I would like to tell you why I took up the practice of sea swimming all year round.

The Irish seas are generally cold all year round. Ranging from a minimum of 2oC in winter and a maximum of 10oC in summer. However, on average it is around 6oC most of the year.

In order to be more mindful, I took up sea swimming. When you swim in the sea at any time of the year it focuses your mind very sharply. The initial shock of the cold water wakes you up. You cannot think of anything else. While you are swimming you are constantly conscious of your surrounding such as other water users, what way is the wind blowing, is there a current, are the waves influencing my direction of travel, the beautiful views from the sea of the hinterland and horizon, the magic of the light from the sea especially during sunrise or sunset, the wind blowing on your face, the waves crashing on your back, that glow feeling of your core body warming up while in the cold water. It is a heightened state for the senses.

And when you get out of the water, the senses again go through several feelings from wind chill on wet skin, to drying off, to the warming feeling of putting dry clothing on again and the joy of a hot drink or food afterward. Often the good sensation of the swim will continue throughout the day. You also get a greater appreciation of how your body can adapt to different situations.

All of these senses are heightened from a single sea swim. I am acutely aware of all of these senses as they are happening. This for me is a mindful state. My other thoughts and worries are temporarily suspended.

Other Examples of Daily Mindfulness Habits

Eat mindfully

We lead busy lives and often rush our food or eat while we are doing something else such as watching our computer, phone or TV. You could instead really focus mindfully on your food and focus on the different colours, textures and smells and take time to saviour each mouthful.

Spend time outside

Spending time outside anywhere can be a great opportunity to practice mindfulness. All you have to do is take a walk around your neighbourhood. While you are walking pay particular attention to your surroundings using as many of your senses as possible. Observe what you see on your walk, feel the wind/sun on your skin, feel your steps on the ground, stop to hear the sounds around you and any smells around you. It is good to stop from time to time to pay particular attention to one or other of your senses.

Get in to flow states as often as possible.

Flow states are states of total absorption, you are so engrossed in the activity that you lose tract of time. This is usually when you are fully engaged in a favourite sport or hobby. This means you are truly present.

Feel your Feelings

Being mindful is being more aware of yourself in the present moment. This can include focusing your attention on your current feelings in the present moment and be just aware of those emotions whether good or bad. Try not focus on whether they are good or bad just be aware of the emotion as a mindful exercise. Observe your feelings as passing ships.

Be Creative

Mindfulness can create space for creative ideas to arise. Also, when you are being creative whether in a hobby or doing something you love is a good opportunity to be mindful as you will often be very focused on the activity and this in its own right is an opportunity to practice mindfulness and be present.

5.2.5 Try These to Improve Your Attitude to the Present

A. Observe the mind Pay attention to your thoughts especially of the past or future, do not judge them just observe, this observation alone withdraws the energy from it. To free your mind of time is to free your need to allow your past to define your identity or your future for fulfilment. Pay close attention to whatever you are doing in the moment, see yourself as an external observer of the activity paying very close attention to the senses if the mind wanders bring it back and never look back unless you want to go that way.

B. Make Practicing Meditation a daily habit for a week, and continue the practice if you feel some benefit, you may need to practice for more than a week to feel the real benefit.

C. Make Practicing Mindfulness a daily habit for a week, and continue the practice if you feel some benefit, you may need to practice for more than a week to feel the real benefit.

D. To improve performance stop thinking about it.

E. Relish or Saviour what you are doing in the present using as many of your senses as possible.

F. Get in to flow states as often as possible. Flow states are states of total absorption, you are so engrossed in the activity that you lose tract of time. This means you are truly present.

G. Consider life as a journey of moments in the present.

5.3 Attitude to Goals

"The trouble with not having a goal is that you can spend your life running up and down the field and never score."
Bill Copeland

"You can't hit a target you can't see. You can't accomplish wonderful things with your life if you have no idea of what they are. You must first become absolutely clear about what you want if you are serious about unlocking the extraordinary power that lies within you."
Brian Tracey

5.3.1 What is Attitude to Goals

Attitude to Goals is a your approach to setting, generating and achieving goals in your Life.

Goals are specific targets that we set out to achieve over a specific time.

Unfortunately, we as humans are not very good at achieving our goals. In his book "Success Principles" Jack Canfield states that one research study has shown that only 8% of people stuck to their new Years' resolutions.

5.3.2 Why is Attitude to Goals Important

Goals are really important to set and strive for if we want to get what we want. They give us purpose and direction. Without goals we can often drift aimlessly. A longitudinal study in Harvard University in 1953 followed graduates over a 25-year period. The study followed two sets of graduates. The ones who had set goals and the ones that did not have goals set. Only 3% of the study group reported as having set goals.

The finding of the study found after 25years that the goal-setting group had more stable marriages, had better health and were worth more financially than the 97% put together.

Covey the author of "7 Habits of Highly Effective People" found that Goal setting was one of those 7 habits. He called it Beginning with the end in Mind.

If you were asked to hit a target with a bow and arrow but could not see the target. What is the likelihood of hitting the target ? The answer is very unlikely.

The same is true of achieving the things you want in life. You have to be able to be very specific about what you want. There are many books dedicated to this topic alone. Most of the management theorists agree that any Goal has to be at least SMART. George T. Doran coined this rule in 1981 in a management research paper of the Washington Power Company and it is by far one of the most popular propositions.

Jim Rohn, author and multimillionaire, was asked by his mentor how he was getting on. He asked him for a copy of his goals. Jim said he did not have them. His mentor pressed him further by asking were they in his car or at home. Jim had to admit at 25 he did not have any list of Goals. His mentor said this was the main reason why Jim was not successful at that time. Jim puts his subsequent success down to setting and pursuing specific goals from that moment on.

The "Action for Happiness" movement says that setting goals contributes considerably to happiness and is one of the movement's 10 keys to Happiness called Direction. This has been empirically proven by many major studies which can be access from this movement's website.

https://www.actionforhappiness.org/10-keys-to-happier-living/have-goals-to-look-forward-to/details

5.3.3 Advice for your Attitude to Goals

- You can't hit a target you cannot see, goals are essential for happiness and purpose.

- SMARTER goals should be set where possible.

- Use the Following to help you generate your Goals (see 5.3.5)
  - Goal Wheel
  - Use the Regrets of the Dying
  - Set Big Goals
  - Use the Rocking chair Method
  - Use Your Values
- Follow the Goal Setting Advice outline in this section (see 5.3.6)

- Follow the Goal Achievement advice as set out in this section (see 5.3.7)

5.3.4. Smarter Goals

S-M-A-R-T goals stand for:

- S (Specific) – They target a particular area of functioning and focus on building it. E.g., My weight is 80kg.

- M (Measurable) – The results can be gauged. This helps in monitoring the progress after following the plans. E.g., 80Kg. The results should be real but can include feelings. E.g. I will feel more confident

- A (Attainable/Achievable) – The goals are targeted to suit different people and are individualized. They take into account the fact that no single rule suits all, and are flexible in that regard. E.g. Currently I weigh 89Kg so the goal of 80 Kg for me is attainable

- R (Realistic) – They are practical and planned in a way that would be easy to implement in real life. E.g. lifestyle change and diet has been proven scientifically to reduce weight.

- T (Time-bound) – An element of time makes the goal more focused. It also provides a time frame for task achievement. My weight is 80Kg in 6 months' time.

While this was the golden rule of goal-setting, researchers have also added two more constituents to it, and call it the S-M-A-R-T-E-R rule.

The added adjacents are:

- E (Evaluative/ethical) – The achievement of the goal follows professional and personal ethics. Eg, I do not use unethical practices or unsafe practices to lose the weight against my values and beliefs and professional best practice.

- R (Rewarding) – The end-results of the goal-setting comes with a positive reward and brings a feeling of accomplishment to the user. E.g. I will plan a weekend away after the achievement of the goal.

Example of a SMARTER Goal

I weigh (S) 80Kg (M, A, R) in 6 months (T) from today. This will be done by diet and lifestyle changes in line with professional advice and according to my beliefs (E). On achieving this goal, I will be rewarded with a weekend away in The Wicklow Bay Hotel (R).

5.3.5 Advice for Generating Goals

1. Use a Goal Wheel

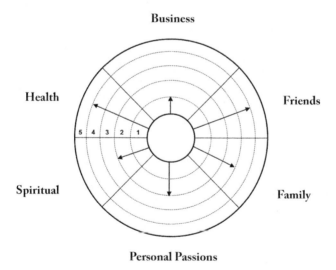

In order to generate goals in all the areas of your life it may be good to start with your Goal Wheel: To do this rate these areas of your life on a scale from 1 to 5 (1 being extremely dissatisfied, 5 being extremely satisfied).

Business: How do you feel about your work, career or business effectiveness and success?

Friends: How is your social life and friendships?

Family: How are your family relationships? Your partner or spouse?

Personal Passions: Do you have personal passion projects, hobbies, or fun activities that fulfil you?

Spiritual: It could be your faith, mental health, personal journeys or mindset.

Health: Are you happy with your physical health and wellness?

A finished Goal Wheel will have the lines filled in so you can see what your 'emotional temperature' is in each area. For example, this is my Wheel right now. You can see I may need to focus my goals on Business, Passions and Spirituality as priorities as these are the lowest on the Wheel. A finished Goal Wheel will have the lines filled in so you can see what your 'emotional temperature' is in each area.

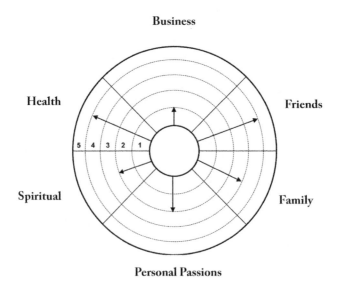

2. Consider Some of the Regrets of the Dying when setting Goals

Bonnie Ware is an Australian nurse who spent several years working in palliative care, caring for patients in the last 12 weeks of their lives. She recorded their dying epiphanies in a blog called Inspiration and Chai, which gathered so much attention that she put her observations into a book called "The Top Five Regrets of the Dying."

Ware writes with great clarity of vision that people gain at the end of their lives, and how we might learn from their wisdom. "When questioned about any regrets they had or anything they would do differently," she says, "common themes surfaced again and again."

Here are the top five regrets of the dying, as witnessed by Ware:

- I wish I'd had the courage to live a life true to myself, not the life others expected of me. This was the most common regret of all. Near death Ware says that most people had not honoured even half of their dreams and they realised that this was due to the choices they had made, or not made.

- I wish I hadn't worked so hard. They regretted missing time that could be spent with their family.

- I wish I'd had the courage to express my feelings. They often supressed their feelings. This often stifled their development and true potential.

- I wish I had stayed in touch with my friends. Often people regretted letting true friends slip away.

- I wish that I had let myself be happier. Deep regrets were expressed on not being happier and often patients expressed that they pretended to be content to others but fear of change and familiarity prevented true happiness.

What is your greatest regret so far, and what will you set out to achieve or change before you die? Review these common regrets when you are setting your Goals to get the inspiration to not have too many life time regrets.

3. Set Big Goals

Sometimes these are called Dreams. A TEDx speaker Keiarna Cove says that

> *"If people are not laughing at your Goals, they are not big enough to be a Dream."*

She states that Goals can often be too specific and narrow your vision. Whereas Dreams are very Big but are very adaptable. She gives an example in her own career where she set a very specific goal of working for a local petroleum company. However, she later changed that Goal to a broader dream to be able to describe the chemical reaction of petroleum in water with sunlight and pave the way to solving the global issue of oil spillages. She eventually found the Petroleum Company she wished to work for were now seeking her advice.

4. Use the Rocking Chair Method

This is a technique where you imagine you are sitting in a rocking chair near the end of your life and are thinking over how you have lived and what have you become and what have you achieved. What would you want to be remembering that was positive?

5. Use your Values to set Goals

We saw in chapter 3 how important values are to us. These values provide guidelines to us on how to live. The research has shown that if we live in alignment with our values we will be most satisfied. Hence it is useful to consider our values when setting our goals. If family is an important value then we should set goals which honour this value. For example – I set a goal to visit my mother three times a week for the next year because my family value is important to me.

It is helpful to put your values into practice by setting goals that put your values into practice.

5.3.6 Advice for Goal Setting

- Personalise the Goal, Use the personal "I "in the goal e.g. " I am 80Kg", "I earn €100K", this personalises the goal and promotes more ownership.

- Always use the present tense when setting goals, do not use "I will be 80Kg" instead use the present moment in the goal "I am 80Kg"

- Always write goals in the positive, e.g., instead of saying "I want to lose 9kg", instead say "I am 80kg" or if the goal is I want to quit smoking, say "I am a non-smoker."

- When setting goals always ask the Why question in relation to the goal. It is more likely the goal will be achieved if the reason for the goal's achievement is clear. Ask yourself why the goal matters. Alignment of your goal to a Core Values and Beliefs can lead to better commitment. E.g. "I want to lose the weight because I want to be healthier for my children, so I can participate and spend more active time with them." Make sure you write down beside your goal the Why of your goal.

- Identify what emotions are associated with the goal. The more feelings and emotions associated with the goal the more likely it will be achieved. The purpose of every goal is to experience a feeling or emotion. We need to spend time considering how you will feel when you achieve the goal. Also, the more senses we can use to get a sense of what will happen when we achieve the goal the better. What will we see, what will we hear how will we feel?

- Questions. Goals are often best broken down into questions to break them up into achievable chunks that move you in the right direction toward your Goal. This ensures you focus on the behaviours needed for achievement of the Goal and not solely the final target. Sometimes this is referred to as reverse engineering where the goal is broken into small tasks to make them more achievable. Questions help this process.

E.g. Goal "I am earning 100K in my own business by next year."

Write at least 20 questions to how the goal can be achieved e.g.

- ❑ Where can I seek out new customers?
- ❑ Do I need to upskill?
- ❑ Do I need to read more about how to earn more?
- ❑ When will I Brainstorm ideas for earning more cash?
- ❑ Do I need to Setup a new website?
- ❑ Will I need to contact social media companies?
- ❑ When will you get mentor?
- ❑ When will I launch a new Marketing Campaign?
- ❑ Do I need to list 3 people who owe me a favour and contact them?
- ❑ etc

It is often the 20th question that might move you in the right direction.

- Set goals you think have only 60% chance of achieving not 100%. The fear of failure can be a motivating factor suggests author Dr Beecham. If it is 100% achievable then your goals are too easy.

- Set Flourishing Goals for personal growth which are not driven by basic need.

5.3.7 Advice for Goal Achievement

1. **Ensure you read over your goals every day.** It is very useful to review your goals daily so that you can prioritise your daily activities. If the activity is not advancing one of your goals it may not be a priority.

2. **Do something every day to progress the goals.** You must be action-oriented. But in particular try to ensure you have done something (behaviours above), no matter how small to move you closer to your goal. It can be useful to record this in your journal under a specific heading such as Goal Advancement or for short GA or you could tick off the behaviours above when completed. Record what you did in relation to which goal, e.g.,

under GA in your Journal record for example "purchased a book on investments to progress my Financial Independence Goal".

3. **Do not make excuses for not doing things to progress your goals.** When people are progressing goals often, they put off advancing the goal by saying they will do it Someday and give all kinds of excuses for delaying. I am too old, too small, too tall, I haven't got enough time, I haven't got enough money etc. Author of the book "Maximum Achievement" Brian Tracey refers to this as going on holiday to a very popular resort called "Someday Isle". Do not be the one who holidays on "Someday Isle".

4. **Visualisation helps make goals more concrete and achievable as you have a clear vision of what you want to achieve.** Some people use Vision Boards with a mixture of pictures, words, diagrams of their goals achieved which is kept in a prominent place to remind them of what they want. Keith Earl, the Irish Rugby player, in his autobiography "Fight or Flight" states that he used Visualisation to turnaround his performances where he practiced visualising playing set pieces both well and not so well, so that when they actually happened, he had already worked through them. He also said he set Goals for himself using Visualisation and was amazed when they came through exactly as he had visualised them.

5. **Use the power of the law of attraction.** The process is explained as simple. It is a three-part process. 1. Ask for what we want (Goal). Believe in your heart and thoughts that you have it, really feel with your senses having received what you want. The Universe will/may provide from here. As Jim Rohn says "Asking starts the receiving process"

6. **Break the Big Goals down into smaller pieces.** You could use the image of how do you eat an elephant, the answer being one small piece at a time. Joe Barr the Endurance Cyclist in his book "Going the Distance" says he uses this approach when doing very challenging long-distance cycling events including the Across America Cycling Challenge. He does not focus on the big challenge but focuses on smaller destinations along the way.

Will Smith in his autobiography "Will" 2021 uses another example of this approach. His father tasked his sons to build a wall in front of his shop. This task was enormous as it was a huge wall to build. His father demolished the old wall and set about getting his sons to build a new replacement using small bricks. His father only supervised the project and the two brothers had to do everything else from mixing the mortar to laying each brick. The brothers thought this was an impossible task which took a full year of work almost every day. But brick by brick the wall was built after almost a year of hard continuous work.

When the sons were complaining of the enormity of the task his father would say to them.

"Stop thinking about the damn wall…. there is no wall. There are only bricks, your job is to lay this brick perfectly. Then move on to the next brick. Then lay this brick perfectly. Then the next one. Don't be worrying about no wall. Your only concern is the one brick." - Daddio Smith

Will reflects on the lesson his father was trying to give his sons

"For my entire career, I have been absolutely relentless. I've been committed to a work ethic of uncompromising intensity. And the secret to my success…you show up and you lay another brick. Pissed off? Lay another brick. Bad opening weekend? Lay another brick.

Album sales dropping get up a lay another brick. Marriage failing? Lay another brick."- Will Smith

7. **Love the Process When trying to achieve a goal you need to love the process. There are three parts to goal achievement.** 1. You set the goal you want to achieve, 2. You need to put in train a process to achieve the goal 3. You achieve the Goal

The most important thing to do is love the process. So, if you want to get fitter, you join a gym class which is the process. This process will get you to achieve the goal but is often the stumbling block. To avoid this, you need to love this process by telling yourself it is great as it will get you to your Goal. It may be painful but you love it because it will get you there. Some people bring their favourite music along to make it more enjoyable.

5.3.8 Try These to Improve your Attitude to Goals

1. Write out 5 SMARTER Goals you wish to achieve over the next year

2. Use the Goal Generating and Setting Advice from this section to help generate and set your goals properly

3. Once your Goals are written down follow the Goal Achievement advice outlined in this section to achieve these 5 Goals

4. Review the Goals regularly to ensure you are on track.

5.4 Attitude to Gratitude

"Be thankful for what you have; you'll end up having more. If you concentrate on what you don't have, you will never, ever have enough."
Oprah Winfrey

"When you are grateful, fear disappears and abundance appears."
Anthony Robbins

"Acknowledging the good that you already have in your life is the foundation for all abundance."
Eckhart Tolle

"We should certainly count our blessings, but we should also make our blessings count."
Neal A. Maxwell

"We can complain because rose bushes have thorns, or rejoice because thorns have roses."
Baptiste Alphonse Karr

5.4.1 What is Attitude to Gratitude

Attitude to Gratitude is your approach to gratitude which will enhance your Life.

According to the Collins English Dictionary

"Gratitude is a state of feeling grateful, a feeling of thankfulness or appreciation."

5.4.2 Why is an Attitude to Gratitude Important

Being grateful is the one the most powerful tools to improve your happiness, optimism and mental health. The action for happiness

Movement says we need to train our brains to look for what's good because our natural tendency is to focus on what is wrong.

The "Action for Happiness" movement says being grateful contributes considerably to happiness and is one of the movement's 10 keys to Happiness called Emotions. This has been empirically proven by many major studies which can be access from this movement's website. https://www.actionforhappiness.org/10-keys-to-happier-living

5.4.3 Advice for Attitude to Gratitude

We should be grateful for what we have and it is a good idea to write this gratitude down. Gratitude is a key to happiness.

5.4.4 Examples of Attitude to Gratitude

Millionaire Mindset Podcast Example

There is a podcast called the Millionaire Mindset Podcast. The host of the podcast has two guests and he poses a series of questions to them. It goes something like this.

The host says "If I decided to give you $1million cash now how would you feel?"

The first guest said

"I would be delighted because I know what I would do with it."

The second guest says

"I would be delighted. I would be on Cloud Nine."

The Host then says

"If I upped the offer to $10million dollars in cash now but you could not wake up tomorrow you are done tomorrow…would you take it?"

Both guests say they would NOT take it....

The host then launches into the following. "What you both are saying it is worth more than $10 million just waking up!!!"

The guests say "that's a hell of perspective."

The host then says...

"Why aren't you feeling that way every time you wake up? Nobody looks at it this way. We get up we have a bad day... this sucks that sucks... I can't lose weight, the world hates me, I can't make money, it's not fair... blah blah blah..."

He continues to remind his guests that they get the opportunity to wake up... and says

"Oh my God I get to get another one (day)... I get to try some more... it's going to happen this day, and it will eventually, it will when you have this Attitude to Gratitude.............."

Example of using a Gratitude Journal

This is a technique used by many people which involves writing down daily at least 3 things you are grateful for every day. I write down at least 3 things I am grateful for everyday in my Bullet Journal. Dr Spiegelman the father of Positive Psychology is an advocate of this technique and has shown empirical evidence to prove it is beneficial to our happiness and our positive mental health as outlined in his book Flourish.

Writing down 3 things to be grateful for can be difficult at first because of the fact that our mind has a negative bias. However, when we get into this practice the mind will start to actively seek out moments and events to be thankful for. This will counter the negative Bias. It is best practice to record these gratitude lists in a Journal if possible.

Even on a day where everything goes wrong it is still possible to find some things in your day that you can be grateful for. One of the big mistakes is that we raise the bar too high when we are making a Gratitude List at the end of the day. We feel we should only be recording amazing things that have happened and that is ok but we should lower the bar to widen the scope of what we are grateful for. For example the fact that you are alive today is something to be grateful for as over 16000 people die worldwide every day. Ordinary things like getting a good night's sleep, nice weather, a nice meal, good company, an interesting/good film or documentary, helping others or something small going well are all worth recording.

Personal Examples

Here are some examples from my own recordings of Gratitude which I do on a daily basis

Day 1 Example of Gratitude recordings

- I am Grateful to have got Another One day (IGAO)
- Had a nice meal in NICOs with my family
- Weather was very nice sunny and blue skies
- Was of service, helped R
- Sunrise open swim amazing light and views

Day2

- IGAO
- Met my son for coffee, he was in good form
- Enjoyed Interesting film on Netflix "Epic" story of survival in the mountains
- Nice walk in the evening
- Made good progress writing today

Day3

- Met an old friend who I had not seen for 10 years, enjoyed exchanging stories
- Enjoyed open sea swim today in Low Rock, sea was very calm, enjoyed coffee afterwards
- Enjoyed banjo lesson tonight I notice the right hand movements are improving
- IGAO

Day 4

- Was out of my Comfort Zone today – cycled 100km but enjoyed the physical challenge
- Met many new people today on cycling event
- I enjoyed the balloon launch tonight
- IGAO
- Enjoyed soup today – Charred Aubergine and Tomato in TANG

  ETC…

5.4.5 Try This

- At the end of each day for a week record 3 things you are grateful for
- At the end of the week note what affect this exercise has on your happiness, do you find you are seeking out what you can be grateful for during the day.

5.5 Attitude to Creativity

"Imagination is everything. It is the preview of life's coming attractions."
Albert Einstein

"The chief enemy of creativity is good sense."
Pablo Picasso

"The difficulty lies not so much in developing new ideas as in escaping from old ones."
John Milton Keynes

"Creativity is intelligence having fun."
Albert Einstein

5.5.1 What is Attitude to Creativity?

Attitude to Creativity is your approach to Creativity so that it will work for you.

"Creativity is the ability to transcend traditional ideas, rules, patterns, relationships, or the like, and to create meaningful new ideas, forms, methods, interpretations, etc.; originality, progressiveness, or imagination."
Dictionary.com

Creativity involves using our gifts to bring something new into the world through our own imagination.

5.5.2 Why is Attitude to Creativity Important

Everyone is creative but you have to give yourself permission to be creative. Often creative ideas come from the subconscious in our dreams or when our minds are calm (during meditation). Creativity is often said to come from deep sources. Artist often say they sat down and the song/poem/art work came to them from where they do not know. This is important as often creative ideas/works come from your true passions, inspirations and intuition and values.

According to data analysis by Linked In, in 2019 companies were looking most for these soft skills in this rank order.

1. Creativity
2. Persuasion
3. Collaboration
4. Adaptability
5. Time Management

5.5.3 Advice for Attitude to Creativity

- Creativity is bringing our gifts to create something new, creativity can follow a process. Follow a process to help Creativity.

- Lateral Thinking can break the normal thinking patterns to aid creativity. Use Lateral Thinking to help your creativity.

5.5.4 Examples of Attitudes to Creativity

There are many examples of creativity, as creativity can be expressed in many different forms. Listed is a few examples:

1. Artistic creativity such as painting, sculpture, dance, music, theatre, and other forms of creative expression.

2. Scientific creativity such as discovering new insights, developing novel theories, and creating new technologies.

3. Technological creativity such as designing innovative processes, products and systems that solve problems and improve lives.

4. Entrepreneurial creativity such as developing new businesses, products, and services.

5. Social creativity such as new ways of thinking about and addressing social problems, such as poverty, inequality, and environmental issues.

6. Personal creativity such as developing your own unique ideas, talents, and perspectives, writing and journaling.

How to cultivate Creativity- An Example

James Webb Young published a guide "A Technique for Producing Ideas." Young outlines the creative process follows five steps.

The Creative Process

1. Gather new material. During this stage you focus on learning specific material directly related to your task and learning general material by becoming engrossed in a wide range of ideas and concepts.

2. Think about the material in stage 1. You examine the material from different angles.

3. Take a break from the problem. You put the problem out of your mind and go do something else. This is like sleeping on a problem overnight but it usually is a break completely from the project for a longer period.

4. Return to the idea. The hope is when you return to the idea after a break you will have some new ideas and insights.

5. Get Feedback. You need to get feedback so you need to release the creative ideas out into the world, get criticism, or praise and adapt it as needed.

Example of Lateral Thinking as a Cognitive Creative Process

Edward De Bono is the father of creative thinking and the inventor of the phrase Lateral Thinking. In his book "Lateral Thinking" he outlines what Lateral Thinking is. It is also known as thinking outside the box where different methods of thinking are used to generate new ideas or to be creative. Lateral thinking or horizontal thinking encourages longer brainstorming. In contrast traditional vertical thinking tends to go with the first good idea and then launch into details and plans.

An example of Lateral Thinking is given by Do Bono when he came up with a novel solution to a short-term parking problem in a Nordic City. No matter how many parking fines were issued in the short-term parking zone people continued to park there for longer than was allowed. De Bono came up with the novel idea that cars that parked in this zone had to keep their lights on. Normally a battery will only last for 1 hour so the parking issue policed itself without any need for expensive parking machines and tickets and monitoring. If the parked car was left in the short-term parking spot for more than an hour the car would not start. Hence the system was self-regulating.

What are Lateral Thinking techniques?

Edward de Bono proposed four techniques for lateral thinking: awareness, random stimulation, alternatives, and alteration.

Awareness, De Bono says we should first be aware of how our minds process information. The first step toward greater innovation is to resist normal thinking patterns

Random stimulation; Inserting randomness is important to assist Lateral Thinking and this can include looking up random words in a dictionary and using them to assist idea generation, using random activities such as listening to a podcast, having a conversation with a stranger, varying the routes to work.

Alternatives: De Bono encourages us to take more time to think of other options. In his view, it's the only way to truly consider the problem from all angles.

Alteration: Looking at a problem in the reverse way can generate different thinking by going in the opposite direction of what's suggested to see what emerges.

More Information on Lateral Creative Thinking is available here: https://www.edwddebono.com/lateral-thinking

https://www.forbes.com/sites/phillewis1/2020/03/20/the-most-valuable-skill-in-difficult-times-is-lateral-thinking-heres-how-to-do-it/

5.5.5 Try This

1. Try to do something creative or come up with a creative solution to a current problem using the Creative Process Example outlined above.

2. Use the Lateral Thinking Techniques Example method to come up with another solution to the problem in 1. above.

5.6 Attitude to Action

"Be disturbed by your own INACTION ....Ease is the greatest enemy."
Dean Graziosi

"Either you run the day or the day runs you."
Jim Rohn

"If you can't fly then run, if you can't run then walk, if you can't walk then crawl, but whatever you do you have to keep moving forward."
Dr. Martin Luther King Jr.

"I hated every minute of training, but I said, 'Don't quit. Suffer now and live the rest of your life as a champion."
Muhammad Ali

"The world can only be grasped by action, not by contemplation. The hand is the cutting edge of the mind."
Jacob Bronowski

"I have been impressed with the urgency of doing. Knowing is not enough; we must apply. Being willing is not enough; we must do."
Leonardo da Vinci

"Just Do It."
Nike Brand Slogan

5.6.1 What is Attitude to Action

Attitude to action is your approach to taking action in your Life by having a Bias for Action where appropriate.

Action is defined as "the fact or process of doing something typically to achieve an aim" Oxford Languages

A "Bias for Action" refers to an attitude or approach that prioritizes taking action over excessive analysis or planning. It's about being proactive, taking risks, and making decisions quickly in order to achieve results.

5.6.2 Why Attitude to Action is Important

The mind is great at coming up with reasons for not taking action. The brain is designed to keep us safe. For that reason, we are designed to look for risks in order to survive. A bias for action is a habit of taking action over inaction in most situations.

Research shows that those who are able to develop the habit for action are many times more likely to be successful in business and in their relationships than people who describe themselves as procrastinators or are unable to take regular action.

A bias for action can be a valuable quality. It can help individuals or teams to move forward and make progress, even in the face of uncertainty or ambiguity. It can also promote a sense of urgency and a willingness to experiment, which can lead to innovation and growth.

It is important to balance a bias for action with careful consideration. Acting too quickly or without sufficient analysis can lead to mistakes.

5.6.3 Advice for Attitude to Action

- Cultivate a Bias for Action.

- Bias for Action is a habit for taking action over inaction, this bias for action can be improved using the methods/examples described below.

5.6.4 Examples

Developing the Bias for Action habit can be improved:

1. If you have an idea consider it by writing it down

   Consider the pros and cons of the idea. Consider also where the idea is coming from, is it your head/heart intuition or experience. If you think it is worth following you MUST take ACTION. Do not wait until everything is ready. If your take action and it is not working you can always change if needed.

2. Be aware of the Discouragement Committee

   There will always be those who will crush your idea. Be prepared for this and stick to your own intuition but listen to the arguments put forward and consider them.

3. Reducing Distractions

   People say that the main reason for not taking action is that they are too busy.

   If you can reduce the number of things you are doing the better able you are to focus on what really matters. Manage better your time in relation to mobile phone and email use. Practice being selective in what you agree to do.

4. Use the Five-Second Rule

   In the book "The Five Second Rule" by Mel Robbins she describes how she uses the counting from 5 to 1 every time she needed to take action. This idea came from her looking at a rocket launch. This improved her action-taking as it provide a timed launch countdown to any of her action and gave her a brief pause before the action.

5. Make smaller decisions

   The long-term big goals are useful, but they often are not attained unless you make the right smaller decisions on a daily basis.

6. Develop a habit of Action (see section 5.7).

7. Develop the courage to take action by being comfortable with your own Vulnerability.

   One of the most watched TED talks is one from Dr. Bernie Brown called the Power of Vulnerability.

   She argues we need to be open to vulnerability including shame and fear, where there are no guarantees in order for some connections to be opened and for us to be seen.

   It is natural to be vulnerable when we have to do something new or perform in front of different people. We will be nervous and conscious of what others think but if we recognise this vulnerability and accept it we can use it to be a catalyst for taking Action. The vulnerability can be a sign of our authenticity and courage to be seen.

8. Embrace experimentation: Be willing to experiment and try new things. Understand that failure is a natural part of the process and you are not afraid to learn from your mistakes.

9. Focus on speed: Actions are prioritised at speed over perfection. It is sometimes better to make quick decisions and adjust as needed, rather than waiting for everything to be perfect.

10. Encourage risk-taking: By encouraging a culture of risk-taking, you can empower people to make quick decisions and take action when needed.

11. Trust in intuition: Sometimes you need to make decisions based on gut feelings, rather than relying solely on data analysis.

5.6.5 Try This

Consider some thing that you have been putting off recently. Try to put it into action by using some of the techniques above. (see 5.6.4)

5.7 Attitude to Habits

"People make a few small changes, fail to see a tangible result, and decide to stop…habits need to persist long enough to break through.
James Clear

"Habits are the compound interest of self-improvement."
James Clear

"Drop by drop is the water pot filled."
Buddha

"I fear not the man who has practiced 10,000 kicks, but I do fear the man who has practiced one kick 10,000 times."
Bruce Lee

"Motivation is what gets you started. Habit is what keeps you going."
Jim Rohn

"We are what we repeatedly do. Excellence, then, is not an act but a habit."
Will Durant

"You'll never change your life until you change something you do daily. The secret of your success is found in your daily routine."
John C. Maxwell

5.7.1 What is Attitude to Habits

Attitude to Habits is your approach to forming, having and practicing good habits and eliminating bad habits.

"A Habit is a regular tendency or practice."
Oxford Languages

A habit is something we practice on a regular basis such as washing our teeth in the morning and night or meditating every morning or eating excessively if we are upset.

5.7.2 Why is Attitude to Habit Important

It is estimated that around 40% of everything we do on a daily basis is habitual. This means that a large portion of our lives is on autopilot using our habits. So, it is important to evaluate our daily habits and ask are they limiting us of freeing us? are they empowering us or disempowering us? are these habits helping us reach our potential or not?

James Clear in his book "Atomic Habits" gives the analogy in relation to Habits to the bamboo tree which when the seed is planted no plant appears until 5 years but the plant is busy for those five years developing a very extensive root system. After 5 years the plant will appear and within 6 months can grow to 60 feet. The key point is we need to be patient when developing a new habit as the benefits can be slow to show tangible benefits initially but they will eventually appear if we persist.

Habits are the same as the baboo plant in that we don't normally get results straight away. They need to be practiced for some time in order for us to get to the Plateau of Latent Potential. This is the breakthrough point where we see some benefits of the new habit.

Clear outlines some detailed rules and systems in his book to create good habits which include making good habits obvious, attractive, easy, and satisfying and doing the opposite to break bad habits by making them invisible, unattractive, difficult and unsatisfying. Two examples below illustrate the process.

5.7.3 Advice for Attitude to Habits

- Excellence is not an act but found in daily empowering habits, the benefit of habits will only appear if you persist, know how to form good atomic habits, know how to break bad habits.

- Develop a powerful daily habit routine that works for you. Know that we are what we repeatedly do.

5.7.4 Examples

Good Habit Formation Example

For example, if I want to develop a good habit of getting up at 6.00am every morning.

The process might look like....

Making Habit Obvious – Write down your intention, "I will get up at 6.00am every day for the next 2 months at home"

Making Habit Attractive – I am writing a book and need to get more done without any distractions from others at home, most people in the house are not up before 8.00am so that gives me 2 hours of undisturbed time.

Making Habit Easy – I will have the heater/cooler on at 5.30am so the house is warm/cool getting up

Making Habit satisfying – Have my favourite coffee once I get up, when I complete 30 days in a row of doing this habit give myself a special gift/ meal/ treat

Breaking a Bad Habit Example

For example, if I want to break a bad habit of emotional eating. eating unhealthy food when I am upset and not hungry.

The process might look like....

Making Habit Invisible – Remove any cues in the environment by removing any unhealthy food from the house

Making Habit Unattractive –Focus on the benefits of avoiding this habit, this will ensure I do not go into a spiral of eating unhealthy food and feeling worse about myself after eating it and making me more upset.

Making Habit Difficult – When you get upset before doing anything else go for a walk for 15 minutes.

Making Habit Unsatisfying – Tell others in the family about the bad habit and ask them to call you out if they see you eating the unhealthy food.

Personal Example

I try to practice these daily habits as much as possible.

1. Have a Morning routine.

This can establish a great start to your day where you are proactive in establishing good habits which set you up for the day. My routine goes something like this (I am currently retired)

- Rise early - no later than 7.00am
- Meditate 17 mins (see Appendix 1)
- Exercise -Cardio (walk dog/swim/run) 30 mins min

- Exercise -Resistance = min 15 mins
- Call out my most updated Affirmation List (see 5.1 above)
- Eat a healthy breakfast plant base where possible
- Review Bullet items for the day in the Bullet Journal (see 5.4 above)

2. Have an End of Day Routine

- Review items in my Bullet Journal
- Goals/Life Purpose/Value/Quotations/Bucket List/ (see 5.3 above)
- Set activity (bullets) list in the Bullet Journal for the next day using two key questions, is it essential and does it matter? (See 5.4)
- Record Gratitude (see 5.4) items and Learning Points in my Bullet Journal

3. Be aware of my Thoughts regularly throughout the day and use ANTI ANTs where appropriate. I remind myself of this practice by having my watch/phone beep on the hour and I then consciously review my thinking. (See 5.1 above). Remind myself I am not my thoughts.

4. Think how I can Serve in any situation (see 7.1)

5. Think Win/Win in any relationship/interaction (see 7.2)

6. Live in the Present as much as possible using all my senses and Meditation and Mindfulness Techniques (see 5.2)

7. Practice Forgiveness/Letting Go daily if necessary (see 7.4)

8. Practice Creativity where possible (see 5.5)

9. Learn something new and record any significant learning in a day (see 6.7)

10. Have a Bias for Action (see 5.6)

11. Seek/Ask for Help if needed (see 7.6)

12. Enhance my relationships and connections with people (see 7.5)

13. Engage in Soul enhancing activities by tuning in to my passions, gut feelings, inspirations, values, attitudes and Life Purpose. (see 3.3)

14. Seize opportunities as they arise and take action if appropriate .(see 6.2)

15. Plan for and engage in challenges outside my Comfort Zone (6.3) and see the positive in adversity where possible. (see 6.1)

16. When communicating be aware of the importance of non-verbal cues (see 6.5)

17. Use 30% of disposable income for tiding (10%), passive capital (10%) and active capital (10%) projects. (see 7.3) where possible18. Have a positive attitude to change daily (see 6.3). Remind myself that Fear is ok but is problematic if it stops me from living my life. Fear can be managed by awareness and changing my thoughts. (see 6.6)

5.7.5 Try This

1. Using the examples given above to construct your own Daily Habits Routine. Write it down.

2. Over time adjust your daily habits due to changes in circumstances or goals to ensure maximum benefits

5.8 Key Take Aways regarding Attitudes to Self

- 7 key attitudes to self are analysed in detail which are essential for happiness and fulfilment and being your Best Possible Self.

- Attitude to self-talk is your approach to your inner voice, it can be negative or positive, positive self-talk can be empowering and can be improved with affirmations, negative self-talk is very common and damaging and automatic these are called Automatic Negative Thoughts ANTs, ANTS can be challenged and improved by using several powerful antidotes as outlined in section 5.1 called ANTi ANTs.

- Attitude to the Present, try to live in the present moment as much as possible, we should be the observer of our minds and observe any future or past thoughts which are not in our best interest. Methods of staying present include, observing the mind, practicing meditation and mindfulness, relish and saviour in the present, get in to flow states and consider life as a journey of moments.

- Attitude to Goals, you can't hit a target you cannot see, goals are essential for happiness and purpose. SMARTER goals should be set where possible. Follow the guidelines for setting and achieving goals outlined.

- Attitude to Gratitude, we should be grateful for what we have and it is a good idea to write this gratitude down. Gratitude is a key to happiness

- Attitude to Creativity, Creativity is bringing our gifts to create something new, creativity can follow a process.

Lateral Thinking can break the normal thinking patterns to aid creativity.

- Attitude to Action, a bias for Action is a habit for taking action over inaction, this bias for action can be improved.

- Attitude to Habits, Excellence is not an act but found in daily empowering habits, the benefit of habits will only appear if you persist, know how to form good atomic habits, know how to break bad habits. Develop a powerful daily habit routine that works for you. Know that we are what we repeatedly do.

CHAPTER 6

EXAMINING YOUR KEY ATTITUDES TO SITUATIONS

Introduction

Attitude is how you treat yourself, others and how you approach situations based on your values and beliefs

Attitudes to situations are the attitudes in the definition above which refer to "how you approach situations". These are attitudes in common key situations or circumstances and how you approach these circumstances which in my opinion and many expert's opinions are the best attitude to have in each key situation.

I will be describing these Attitudes to Situations in detail in this Chapter. They include the following

- Attitude to Failure and Difficulty
- Attitude to Opportunity
- Attitude to Change
- Attitude to Productivity
- Attitude to Communication
- Attitude to Fear
- Attitude to Learning

Putting these Key Attitudes to situations into practice will help you greatly on your own journey to becoming your Best Possible Self.

For each Attitude to Situations I will describe the following:

- What is the Attitude
- Why it is Important
- What advice is given for this Attitude
- Examples of this Attitude in use
- Try This yourself

6.1 Attitude to Failure and Difficulty

"Failure is simply the opportunity to begin again,
this time more intelligently."
Henry Ford

"It is never a tragedy to try something and fail
the real tragedy is not to try."
Bill Cullen

"If children gave up when they fell for the first time,
they would never learn to walk."
Louise Hay

"Ease is the greater threat to progress than hardship."
Denzel Washington

"Obstacles Instruct not Obstruct."
Colin Turner

"If you're not failing, you're not pushing your limits, and if you're not
pushing your limits, you're not maximising your potential."
Ray Dalio

6.1.1 What is Attitude to Failure and Difficulty.

Our Attitude to Failure and Difficulty is how we approach both failures and adversity in our lives.

Failure is the lack of success, or the neglect or omission of expected or required action. Such as failing an examination by not passing it, failing to reach a goal by not attaining it or failing to find something.

Difficulty is a difficult or unpleasant situation such a bereavement or personal tragedy such as an accident or illness.

6.1.2 Why your Attitude to Failure and Difficulty is Important

Failures, setbacks and difficulties are going to happen all of us at some point in our lives. We must recognise this and be able to deal with this inevitable reality of Life.

In a now famous Commencement speech Denzel Washington gave to University of Pennsylvania graduates in 2011

"You will fail at some time in your life, accept it, you will embarrass yourself, you will suck at something."

In acting Washington says you fail all the time when going to auditions,

"Here's the thing I did not quit, I continued to fail and fail and fail…. you eventually will catch a break."

Reggie Jackson struck out 2600 times in his career the most in the history of Baseball but you do not hear about the strikeouts people remember the home runs. He continues in his speech.

"Everybody has…. talent to succeed but do you have the guts to fail? ….it may be frightening it may also be rewarding because the chances you take, the people you meet, the people you love, the faith you have that's what going to define you. Keep working keep striving never give up fall down 7 times, get up 8."

According to Denzel if you don't fail you are not even trying, he says failure is sometimes your best path he dropped out of college and got in to acting afterwards.

We all must learn how to deal with difficulties in our life because they are inevitable and will appear at some stage of our life. Jim Rohm calls this our Winters. These can take the shape of economic, personal or social Winters or difficulties. The Winters cannot be changed but You can. You need to prepare for tough time and situations by being stronger, wiser and prepared.

"Smooth seas do not make skilful sailors"
African proverb

Tony Robbins from his Date with Destiny Introduction says

Everyone is going to have difficulty in their life... We all go through extreme stress or difficulty such as health issues, losing a job, having a stressful job.

Learn how to use the stress rather than it use you.

People think if they have no problems, they will be happy... not true ... biggest problem is we think we should have no problems... problems are a sign of life we should let it drive us and let us grow.

You should embrace the fear of failure.

Too much fear of failure can hinder success, but too little fear can demotivate.

The Stoics, the ancient Roman philosophers, saw difficulties as an opportunity for growth, as a means of testing themselves and strengthening their virtues. We need to stop seeing difficulties as a barrier and instead start seeing it as the path for growth that can be taken.

"No tree which the wind does not often blow against is firm and strong; for it is stiffened by the very act of being shaken, and plants its roots more securely: those which grow in a sheltered valley are brittle:"
Seneca

"You are unfortunate in my judgment, for you have never been unfortunate. You have passed through life with no antagonist to face you; no one will know what you were capable of, not even you yourself."
Seneca

When we think about difficulties as an opportunity, we can change the perception of adversity. No obstacle can then lead to despair. People may have to find their own way to create adversity such as physical challenges such as mountain climbing, marathons etc.

Seneca advises us to regularly practise adversity, so we are not taken by surprise when it lands on our doorstep:

"It is in times of security that the spirit should be preparing itself for difficult times."

We don't control external events but we do have control over our reactions to these events.

Victor Frankl was stoic in his approach to finding meaning and his development of a new Therapy from a long period of hardship in a German concentration camp.

Stoics distinguish between things that are under our control and that are outside of our control. Under our control are; our thoughts, our beliefs, and attitude and those outside our control is most other things.

It is best to focus on what we can control, rather than wasting energy on what we cannot control

Ryan Holiday's, "The Obstacle Is the Way" is an excellent book on the Stoic approach. The author outlines 3 key main points in this book.

Perception is important

"There is no good or bad without us; there is only perception. There is the event itself, and the story we tell ourselves about what it means."
Ryan Holiday.

Our perception of an event will determine how we feel about it. If I perceive an event to be difficult then I might feel helpless. So, I may not do anything. If I perceive an event to be difficult, but I decide to find some way to make it better I may feel like doing something about it. Sometimes it is helpful to observe an event as neither good or bad but view it objectively.

Your Power

> *"Focusing exclusively on what is in our power magnifies and enhances our power."*
> Ryan Holiday

We should try and focus on what we control as often we cannot change our circumstances.

This is what he states is under our control and our power

- Our thoughts
- Our perspectives
- Our attitude
- Our creativity
- Our emotions
- Our effort
- Our determination
- How we spend our time

Difficulty

"Yes, it's supposed to be hard, and that doesn't mean you are doing it wrong. Just keep going. "You will fail. Failure is teaching us something. It's teaching us what isn't the way."
Ryan Holiday

In relation to Failure and Difficulties the Stoics advocate Resilience (finding ways to bounce back) and again the "Action for Happiness" movement says that those who find ways to bounce back are happier and is one of the movement's 10 keys to Happiness. This has been empirically proven by many major studies which can be access from this movement's website. https://www.actionforhappiness.org/10-keys-to-happier-living/find-ways-to-bounce-back/details

Resilience can be important to deal with adversity. 3 strategies are outline in a powerful TEDx Talk. by Lucy Hone called Three Secrets of Resilient People.

1. We must remember that suffering and adversity are part of life. We don't welcome it in but we should not be surprised by it because at some point in our life it will emerge. We will often ask why is this happening to me. Lucy Hone says we could say why not me as it is part of life. Social media shows only the positive side of people's lives but everyone has another side.

2. It is good to choose your attention on things that you can change, We are hard-wired to pay attention to negative emotions. We need to pay more attention to the good we need to find what to be grateful for (as discussed in detail in section 5.4 above).

3. We must ask when dealing with adversity is this action I am doing right now in reaction to the adversity serving me or harming me. Lucy Hone gives a personal example when her daughter was killed in a car accident. She asks the question should she meet the driver who killed her… she concludes this would harm her more…

Ray Dalio in his book "Principles" says that one of his Principles for Success is to see Pain of any sort as helping progress. He uses the formulae

Pain + Reflection = Progress

He says we can learn a lot from our pain and adversity and we need to reflect on the pain and what it is teaching us. He says that Life is a continuous set of cycles of facing our challenges and reflecting on them and designing a plan to moving on and finally taking action.

6.1.3 Advice for our Attitude to Failure and Difficulty

- Failure can be seen as the First Attempt at Learning, We can view our response to failure as providing feedback, failure offers a unique opportunity to learn something you might otherwise have missed.

- Practice reframing which is a technique used to deal with disappointments or failure. That is we try to look at failure in a different way such as an opportunity to learn. Also by reframing we can see setbacks not as personal failures where we do not rate ourself as a failure but it is better to rate the behaviour as needing improvement. Reframing can be improved by considering the analogy of stress or disruption as an opportunity to grow. The example sighted often is the where somebody is lifting weights, this stresses the muscles which in turn encourages growth and strength.

- Adversity can make us stronger, we need to be comfortable with adversity as it is part of life, but in order to truly live our lives, we must let go of all those expectations and realize that it's ok to fail sometimes and that doesn't affect our value or the love and support other people have for us.

- Adversity can be practiced in preparation for the inevitability of it, we need to focus on what we can control. We cannot control everything that happens us in life but we can control our response to anything that happens to us good or bad as we saw in Chapter 2 in section 2.4. The Formulae below is a good way to view what we control.

Formulae E + R = O

Where E is an Event or happening

Where R is our Response to the event or happening

Where O is the Outcome (what we do and feel) after the event plus our response.

We can control the R in any given situation.

- We must ask when dealing with adversity is this action I am doing right now in reaction to the adversity serving me or harming me. Focus on the Action that is serving you.

6.1.4 Examples

Take for example Eddison when inventing the light bulb after over 10000 attempts (failures) he succeed in producing a light bulb. His quote:

"I have not failed. I've just found 10,000 ways that won't work. Many of life's failures are people who did not realize how close they were to success when they gave up."
Thomas Edison

Personal Examples

I can reflect on some of the major difficulties in my life, these included the loss of my brother Cathal 20 years ago, the loss of my father Charlie 10 years ago, and my own personal diagnosis of Diabetes 19 years ago........

The loss of a family member is always a very difficult emotional time. Some advice is that we possibly never get over the grief and that is true but the grief becomes more tolerable over time. Those who are left behind often have to re-evaluate their own lives and continue with their lives to honour those who have passed.

My father Charlie's passing was very sad however he was 88 when he passed. His passing was very painful but it was marked in my mind as a celebration of a long life well lived. He dedicated his life to our family and instilled in me and all his family a great love of learning which has stayed with me to this day. I hope in writing this book I can extend Charlie's legacy even further to other people.

The sudden and unexpected passing of my brother Cathal at the age of 42 in 2003 was a huge shock to our family. He died from complications of an Asthma condition whilst living and working as an Engineer in Dubai. He was a hugely talented, fun-loving, generous, intelligent person and professional and was greatly admired by his family, work colleagues and many friends. His passing was a stark reminder to all our family of the fickleness of Life. I know I had to re-evaluate my own life at that time.

You do not truly appreciate adversity and its affects until it knocks on your own door. The personal diagnosis of Diabetes type 1 at the age of 40 years was such a knock on the door for me. I had always kept fit and cycled to and from work everyday for over 15years. I also went hillwalking on most weekends. I also completed the Dublin City marathon in 1998 when I was 35. In relation to nutrition, I was very careful to follow a healthy diet most of the time. So, when I got the diagnosis from a GP I was surprised, disappointed and shocked initially. I was told it was genetic and that my healthy lifestyle possibly helped to keep it at bay.

However, when I had time to assimilate the diagnosis, I had to dig deep to come up with a positive perspective on this. My next youngest brother was a Diabetic Type 1 from the age of 14 so it was definitely in the family. I reasoned to myself that I was lucky to have not had the condition earlier. The other positive was the resolve I mustered up to not let the diagnosis affect my life, in fact it gave me amazing energy to fully understand the condition and help myself to live as my Best Possible Self with the condition. I was very successful at managing my blood sugars over the next decade. I used a minimum number of units of insulin and never had a low sugar incident so much so that after 10 years the doctors took me off insulin and treated my condition instead as type 2/1.5 Diabetes. Currently I am using again a small amount of insulin and mainly lifestyle to manage the condition but it is not affecting the quality of my life. So far so good.

The diagnosis also gave me a wake-up call and I had a sharper focus on what I wanted to do with my life. A year after this I applied for a new job in another City which was a big career promotion. There I had several other promotions including being appointed as CEO of City of Waterford VEC (Waterford ETB) for 4 years. So, on reflection if I had not got that wake-up call, I may not have made that career move. I was getting a taste of Ryan Holidays the Obstacle is the Way.

6.1.5 Try This

- Think of any setback or failure in your life that there was some learning or positive outcome that came of it. This exercise will allow you to see that some setbacks can have a silver lining.

6.2 Attitude to Opportunity

"Opportunity does not knock; it presents itself when you beat down the door."
Kyle Chandler

"Success is where preparation and opportunity meet."
Bobby Unser

"You can so easily fail at what you don't want, so you might as well take a chance of what you love."
Jim Carey

"…opportunities are like buses, there is always another one coming."
Richard Branson

"In a world that is changing really quickly, the only strategy that is guaranteed to fail is not taking risks."
Mark Zuckerberg

6.2.1 What is Attitude to Opportunity

Our Attitude to Opportunity is how we approach opportunities that present themselves in our lives.

According to Dictionary.com an Opportunity is a favourable time or occasion for attainment of a goal or a good position, chance or prospect.

6.2.2 Why an Attitude to Opportunity is Important

We must learn how to take advantage of or seize opportunities when they arise. Jim Rohn refers to opportunities in his book "The Keys to Success" (2013) as the season Spring. Opportunities always come however they need to be taken quickly as they soon run out.

Seizing opportunities can be practiced by the following:

1. Get yourself prepared, Malcolm Gladwell in the book "Outliers" says it takes 10000 hours to be an expert at something. Once you are prepared and expert opportunity has a strange way of showing up.

2. Have Clear Goals. When we have clearly set goals our conscious and subconscious mind are constantly seeking out opportunities to move toward our goals.

3. Seize opportunities quickly as often the opportunity will be taken up by somebody else if we hesitate (see personal example below)

4. The greatest opportunities can often be disguised as our biggest problem. Winston Churchill once famously said "the pessimist sees difficulty in every opportunity, an optimist sees the opportunity in every difficulty" (see personal examples in 6.1 above)

5. Eliminate the Automatic Negative Thoughts and other critical voices to give yourself a chance to isolate every voice or thought. This creates a better mind environment for seeking and finding opportunities.

6. Create more opportunities to meet more people who are different. The more different perspectives, people and experiences you emerge yourself in the more exposed you are to different opportunities.

A good metaphor is that of the Atom where you are randomly bumping in to people which involves transferring energy, bonding and creating something new and progression is not linear but explosive.

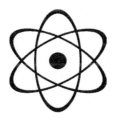

6.2.3 Advice for Attitude to Opportunity

- We must be prepared and attentive to opportunities.
- Opportunities can be seized by
  - Being Prepared
  - Having Clear goals
  - Eliminate ANTs
  - Being Quick to act
  - Opportunities can be disguised as our biggest problem
  - Seek more interaction

6.2.4 Examples

A graduate was looking for a job for months without success. Instead of getting disappointed, this person views their job search as an opportunity to network, build new skills, and gain experience in interviewing and CV writing. They go to job fairs, participate in mock interviews, and volunteer in their community to demonstrate their skills and build their reputation. Their attitude towards opportunity enables them to turn a negative situation into a positive one, and they may get a job they love or discovering a new career path they hadn't considered before.

Personal Example

I remember the opportunity came to write a book with a colleague, Seamus O Neill, very quickly. We were computing teachers and many teachers were contacting us for our notes to help them teach this new subject in the late 1980s. We decide to act fast and approach a publisher. The second publisher we approached agreed to back us and we published Essential Computer Applications by G.Morgan and S.O Neill 6 months after that. This book is currently on its 4th Edition.

6.2.5 Try This

- Record in your Diary or Journal opportunities or ideas that arise on a daily basis.

- Read over these recorded ideas and ideas regularly as they may spark off your Bias for Action at some opportune time.

6.3 Attitude to Change

"It is not the strongest of the species that survives….it is the one that is most adaptable to change."
Charles Darwin

"Failure isn't fatal, but failing to change might be."
John Wooden

"Change can be scary, but it's utterly unavoidable. In fact, impermanence is the only thing that you can truly rely on… The capacity to adjust and improvise is arguably the single most critical human capacity."
Will Smith

"The only thing that is constant is change."
Heraclitus

6.3.1 What is Attitude to Change

Attitude to Change is your approach to change and changing circumstances. Change is a transformation or modification or alteration.

6.3.2 Why is Attitude to Change Important

People in general do not like change and the unknown. This is only natural. However, we have to remember that there is nothing more constant than change. Change is all around us. Every cell in our body is changing all the time. The earth is spinning. The oceans are changing even inanimate objects are changing in subtle ways.

We need to be able to embrace change and see it as a natural process. You can thrive in the process of change. However, the mind sometimes prefers less change and will often resist it to stay in its comfort zone. This again is natural but it may not be in your best interest.

In the book "Who Moved My Cheese" authors Spencer and Johnson, tell the story of 4 characters (mice) who live in a maze and they love cheese (success). Things are constantly changing so they must adapt. The quicker they adapt to change the better. The most successful mice were the ones who

- Accepted and adapted to change

- Anticipated change and got ready for it. Get ready for cheese to move.

- Monitor Change. Smell the cheese often so you know when it is getting old.

- Adapt to change quickly. The quicker you let go of old cheese the sooner you can enjoy new cheese.

- Make that change. Move with the cheese.

- Enjoy change. Enjoy the taste of new cheese.

The same is true of life. Life moves on so should we and embrace change.

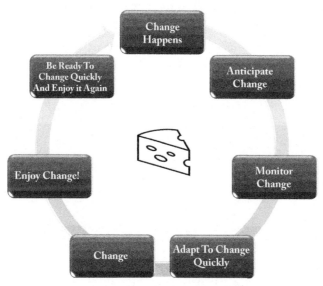

Source: Spenser and Johnstown (1998) *Who Moved My Cheese*

Another way at looking at change is this

Change ⬛≠ **(is not equal to) the end of something**

Change ⬛═ **(is equal to) a new beginning**

6.3.3 Advice for Attitude to Change

- We need to adapt to, enjoy and anticipate change as change is constant. We can prepare for change.

- Change can be seen as a new beginning.

6.3.4 Examples

- A student who has succeeded in school finds that their academic abilities are not enough to succeed in the real world. They must adapt to new challenges and learn new skills to succeed in their career.

- A person who has had a stable relationship suddenly finds that their partner wants to break up. They can either cling to the past and resist the change, or they can accept the change and move on, finding new ways to be happy and fulfilled.

In each of these examples, the central concept of "Who Moved My Cheese?" applies: change is inevitable, and it is up to us to decide how we will respond to it. We can either resist change and cling to the past, or we can adapt and find new ways to succeed in the present and future.

6.3.5 Try This

The author of the book "Emotional Resilience" Dr Harry Barry advocates that we should practice purposely putting change in our lives. This exercise he calls the Coin Test and is based on Cognitive Behavioural Technique CBT method. The test involves:

1. Write down a list of personably enjoyable activities e.g., shopping, watching tv, going to a motive, social media, having a drink, reading a book, social media etc (items must be activities you really enjoy for the exercise to work).

2. For four weeks toss a coin every day to determine which activity you will do. Head means yes tails means no.

The purpose of the exercise is to see how you adapt to things when they don't go your way. What do you do when you are frustrated? How do you change your behaviour, what do you do instead...? this is a "microcosm of real-life."

By the end of the 4-week exercise uncertainty will become the norm. You will no longer seek absolute certainty to more serious concerns because there is no certainty in this life and we have to be able to deal with this.

6.4 Attitude to Productivity

"Focus on being productive instead of busy."
Tim Ferriss

6.4.1 What is Attitude to Productivity

Attitude to productivity is your approach to being productive in your Life.

Productivity is defined as the quality, state, or fact of being able to generate, create enhance or bring forth goods and services (or something of value) Dictionary.com

There is a difference between being busy and being productive. Being busy does not necessarily mean you are being productive. Being productive means, you are doing the things that are essential and doing the things that matter.

6.4.2 Why is Attitude to Productivity Important

When compiling a "to do" list is very important to be productive and this requires us to ask these two key questions:

- Is this activity essential?
- Does this activity matter, i.e., is it aligned to my values, beliefs, attitudes, Life Purpose and Goals?

If the answer to both of these questions is no then the activity is most likely a distraction and should not occupy any of your time and should be removed from your to-do list.

In deciding what is important it is useful to keep in mind Stephen Coveys Time Management Matrix box from his book "First Things First" and the most important quadrant one (I) and two (II) activities he has identified. See the next diagram.

Time Management Matrix

From Stephen Covey's book "First Things First"

	Urgent	Not Urgent
Important	**I** (MANAGE) • Crisis • Medical Emergencies • Pressing Problems • Deadline-driven Projects • Last-minute preparations for scheduled activities **Quadrant of Necessity**	**II** (FOCUS) • Preparation/planning • Prevention • Values clarification • Exercise • Relationship-building • True recreation/relaxation **Quadrant of Quality & Personal Leadership**
Not Important	**III** (AVOID) • Interruptions, some calls • Some mail & reports • Some meetings • Many "pressing" matters • Many popular activities **Quadrant of Deception**	**IV** (AVOID) • Trivia, busywork • Junk mail • Some phone messages/email • Time Wasters • Escape activities • Viewing mindless TV shows **Quadrant of Waste**

6.4.3 Advice for Attitude to Productivity

- We need to be productive not just busy.

- When doing anything we need to ask is it essential, and does it matter i.e., is contributing to and aligned with my beliefs, values and attitudes and your Life Purpose.

- Focus on Quadrant I and II activities (above)

- Use a Bullet Journals to help you be more productive

159

6.4.4 Example

A new approach is emerging to becoming more productive and that is the use of Bullet Journals. This concept was developed by Ryder Carroll. It is basically a technique that uses a journal to write down activities and ideas in an efficient way.

A Bullet Journal (sometimes known as a BuJo) is a method of personal organization developed by designer Ryder Carroll. The system organizes scheduling, reminders, to-do lists, brainstorming, and other organizational tasks into a single notebook. The name "bullet journal" comes from the use of abbreviated bullet points to log information.

The bullet journal system aims to provide a framework for users to plan out their lives and increase productivity. Inherent to the bullet journaling system is flexibility - there is plenty of room for users to customize the system to their needs.

I use a Bullet Journal every day. In the Bullet Journal I have my Goals, My Values, my Affirmations, My bucket List, My Ideas, My favourite quotes and songs, My Purpose, Birthdays of note, Monthly planner and Daily Planner. These are reviewed and updated regularly and there is space in the journal for that.

The journal also has daily and monthly tasks spaces.

The daily tasks are coded thus:

• A dot for a task

o A clear dot for an activity

X over the dot when the activity or event is complete

» Over a dot if the task or event needs to be moved

! to the left of a dot to note a very important task or activity

Also, daily I record in the Bullet Journal

- What I am Grateful for (min 3)

- What went well

- What could have gone better and associated thinking

- Lessons Learned today

- Goal Advancement activities started or completed today code GA

6.4.5 Try This

1. Purchase a blank A4 diary

2. Follow the Instructions of how to set up a Bullet Diary by following Ryder Carroll's talk *"How to Bullet Journal"* on YouTube

6.5 Attitude to Communication

"Effective Communication is 20% what you know and 80% how you feel about what you know."
Jim Rohn

"If you don't have something nice to say, don't say anything at all."
Thumper from the film Bambi

6.5.1 What is Attitude to Communication

Attitude to Communications is your approach to Communications that serves you best in your life.

"Communications is the imparting or interchange of thoughts, opinions or information by speech, writing or signs."
Dictionary.com

6.5.2 Why is Attitude to Communication Important

Communication skills are vitally important for any human being and are a key to success and successful human interactions.

There are four main methods of Communication:

1. Verbal Communication which involves using our voices to communicate

2. Written Communications which involves the use of the written words to convey a message.

3. Non Verbal Communication which is where communications are conveyed by the use of non verbal methods such as body language, body posture, gestures, eye contact, facial expressions, touch and the use of space. Surprisingly non-verbal cues are more important (see the following diagram) when used in combination with verbal communication.

4. Visual Communications this involves communicating using pictures, videos and illustrations. We process information much faster via visual methods than the written word.

ELEMENTS OF PERSONAL COMMUNICATIONS

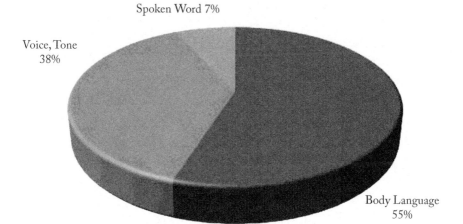

Spoken Word 7%

Voice, Tone
38%

Body Language
55%

Essential Communication Skills

Practice the following to ensure effective communication

1. Being an Active Listening

"The reason why we have two ears and only one mouth is so we might listen more and talk less."
Diogenes Laertius

This means paying very close attention to the speaker by ensuring you get the true essence of what the speaker is saying. It means giving your undivided attention to the person and being fully present and aware of the person and being accepting of them. Giving somebody you full undivided attention is one of the greatest gifts you can give anyone. Active Listening involves some of the following :

- Clarifying, It means you use clarifying questions when needed to ensure you fully understand what is being said. Often the Active Listener will paraphrase or summarize the speakers message so that the speaker has a sense that they are understood.

- Reading between the lines of a message can also be a useful skill of the active listener that is interpreting the real message and feelings from the words that are said and communicating this.

- Being aware of non verbal cues is part of being an active listener as this is a very important part of any speakers message as outlined in the diagram above. Awareness by the active listener should focus on the important non-verbal cues such as body language, emotions, eye contact, gestures and posture. For example if the speaker is being very animated when talking about a particular topic this might indicate a higher emotion involved for the speaker.

- Empathy is another trait of the active listener where the listener tries to see and feel the issues from the other persons perspective.

- Allow the speaker to finish without too many interruptions. There is a tendency for people to be thinking about what we want to say next and they are waiting for their turn to speak.

- We often focus only on the relevant content to you, try to avoid this and show genuine interest in all that is being said.

Active listening is a powerful communicative skill that should be practiced frequently.

2. Being Clear and Precise

It is important to be clear in any communication. This will depend on your audience and should avoid any technical language unless the audience has technical knowledge.

Conciseness will make it more likely the message is clear. Too much information or excessive information only distracts from the core message.

Communication to be effective should comply with the 7 Cs rule. The communication should be

- Clear
- Correct
- Courteous
- Concise
- Coherent
- Concrete
- Complete

3. Engaging your audience

Engaging your audience be it an individual or a group, is important to effective communication. Basic ways of engaging your audience include

- Understand the audience and tailor to their needs and knowledge level
- Use questions to encourage interaction and establish understanding of the key messages
- Read the audience to get feedback and be aware of nonverbal cues
- Use metaphors and stories to improve understanding and engagement
- Use a combination of verbal, written and visual communication methods where possible and appropriate.

4. Practice good non-verbal practices and recognise poor non-verbal cues (see examples below)

5. Be Patient

We need to be patient when communicating. We need some time to give people time to answer a question or to allow time to construct their thoughts.

6.5.3 Advice for Attitude to Communication

- Understand that Communication skills are vitally important for any human being and are a key to success and successful human interactions
- Practice being an Effective Communicator by
  - Being an Active Listener
  - Being Clear and Concise

- Engaging Your Audience
- Practice Good Non Verbal Communication and Understand its importance.
- Be Patient

6.5.4 Examples

Examples of the practice of good non-verbal practices and recognition of poor non-verbal cues:

Good Eye Contact:

- Looking at people's eyes.
- Continually scan the group with your eyes
- Looking at the whole group.

Poor Eye Contact:

- Avoiding eye contact.
- Scanning the group too fast or infrequently.
- Only look at a few people or one area

Good Body Movement:

- Positioning yourself so you face the majority of the audience.
- Varying your position.
- Standing with good posture.
- Walking toward people when they speak.

Poor Body Movement:

- Talking to your notes
- Turning your back.
- Standing in fixed positions or slouching.
- Distancing yourself from the audience/person.

Good Gestures and Facial Expressions:

- Using natural gestures.

- Smiling and being animated.

- Conveying emotion.

Poor Gestures and Facial Expressions

- Engaging in distracting behaviour such as looking at your watch, or fumbling.

- Looking disinterested.

- Using negative gestures or expressions.

6.5.5 Try This

Try this "Active Listening." Exercise. Here are the steps:

1. Find a partner and decide on a speaker and a listener.

2. The speaker will choose a topic they want to discuss, such as a problem they are facing, a goal they want to achieve, or something they are excited about.

3. An active listening scorecard can be used to assess how well someone is actively listening during a conversation. Here's an example of a possible scorecard:

Scorecard:

Score 1: Maintains eye contact with speaker Score: 0-1 point (1 point for consistent eye contact, 0 for lack of eye contact).

Score 2: Demonstrates attentiveness and focus Score: 0-1 point (1 point for active listening, 0 for distraction or lack of focus).

Score 3: Avoids interrupting or talking over the speaker Score: 0-1 point (1 point for not interrupting, 0 for interrupting).

Score 4: Uses appropriate verbal and nonverbal cues to indicate understanding Score: 0-1 point (1 point for using appropriate cues, 0 for not using appropriate cues).

Score 5: Asks clarifying questions to confirm understanding Score: 0-1 point (1 point for asking clarifying questions, 0 for not asking clarifying questions).

Score 6: Paraphrases or summarizes what the speaker has said Score: 0-1: point (1 point for paraphrasing or summarizing, 0 for not paraphrasing or summarizing).

Score 7: Provides feedback or validation to the speaker Score: 0-1 point (1 point for providing feedback or validation, 0 for not providing feedback or validation).

Possible Total Score: 0-7 points

4. The total score can be used to evaluate how well someone is actively listening, with a higher score indicating better active listening skills.

6.6 Attitude to Fear

"The brave man is not he who does not feel afraid,
but he who conquers that fear."
Nelson Mandela

"We should all start to live before we get too old.
Fear is stupid. So are regrets."
Marilyn Monroe

"One of the greatest discoveries a man makes, one of his great surprises, is
to find he can do what he was afraid he couldn't do."
Henry Ford

6.6.1 What is Attitude to Fear

Attitude to Fear is our approach to Fear which is constructive.

There are three types of fear

1. Danger Fear: which is fear which is generated when we are threatened with immediate danger to our safety or survival. This is an essential fear as it will ensure that we take action in face of an immediate threat. If a bear is about to charge at you, you need to take immediate action to save yourself.

2. Specific Fear: which is fear related to a specific situation which is not life threatening but which you are fearful of or when a specific situation or thought arises.

3. Background Fear: this fear can be for some people a continuous background sense of fear/anxiety present in their life

6.6.2 Why is Attitude to Fear Important

Fear is natural and healthy.

Fear can be problematic when it stops you from living your life.

Danger Fear is the simplest and is designed to protect us when it is based on some real/actual threat. The other two types of Fear are often more difficult and have the potential to stop us from living our lives.

Specific Fear and Background Fear are often based on perceived threats which are fears based on the possibility of something happening in the future, something that is created in our minds which may not be true.

When fear gets out of control it can take over the mind and your actions and inactions.

Overcoming Specific and Background Fear

1. Realise you are not your thoughts. There is a distance between you and your thoughts. Hence the fear you perceive is not you. Fear is often not because of the issue but because of the minds distortion of the issue you fear. Fear is often referred to by the acronym F.E.A.R. False Evidence Appearing Real.

2. Be aware of your fears and this will give you a higher awareness of your reality beyond fact and fiction and give you access to inner peace

3. Realise that fear is a message to shift, you can expand once you get to the root cause of your fear and walk through and with your fear. Thoughts and projections are often the root cause, and these thoughts can be changed and projections have not happened and are often incorrect and exaggerated. You can manage and control your thoughts hence you can manage your fears.

4. Logically assess your fears. Write them down and critically and logically assess them. Tim Ferris has a way of doing this which he calls Setting Your Fears. This involves asking yourself three things regarding your fears in any scenario 1. The worst-case scenario, 2. What can be done to prevent the worst case and 3. What can I do to repair the damage or ask for help?

5. When fear gets out of control it can snap us and we can become overcome by the fear and we can become dysfunctional. We need to be able to manage it by the use of some of the following daily practices such as Meditation, Affirmations, Tapping.

6. Seek professional help if your Fears are holding you back.

6.6.3 Advice for Attitude to Fear

- Danger Fear is natural and is there to help protect us.

- Specific and Background fear can hold us back and can be overcome to help us be more productive by

  - Knowing you are not your thoughts

  - Be Aware

  - Fear is a message to shift

  - Logically access your fears

  - If fear is out of control seek professional help

6.6.4 Examples

Example 1

"Life begins at the edge of your comfort zone."
Stanford TEDx Yubing Zhang 2015

Yubing tells a story where she is about to jump from the longest bungee jump in the world. She wants to give up at the last minute and wants to quit then sees the quote above on the wall beside her and... she then jumps... during the fall she thinks this is not so scary as it looks...

She says "That thought lead to a whole new world... every time I hear the voice of fear in my head... I can't leave this job because I am not going to find anything better... I am scared of entering a new relationship because I don't want to be hurt again every time I heard that voice, I take a deep breath and say it is not as scary as it looks..."

We are all scared of uncertainty... but it's not as scary as it looks

Yubing's sees life as a constant fight with your comfort zone... you push it, it pushes back. What is the fear that's holding you back? What are you not saying or doing because it is outside your comfort zone? Find it and bravely step out of it and as you get out of it push it further do not try to get rid of fear but accept you will be afraid and go do it anyway.

Example 2

Cognitive-Behavioural Therapy (CBT): CBT is a therapy method that helps a person to identify and challenge negative thoughts and beliefs. By changing these thoughts, a person can reduce their fear and anxiety. For example, someone who is afraid of making a speech might believe that they will embarrass themselves or be judged by others.

Through CBT, they can learn to challenge these thoughts and develop a more positive and realistic attitude.

Example 3

Gradual Exposure: Gradual exposure involves facing the fear in a controlled way where the feared item is gradually introduced to the client. For example, A fear of spiders might begin by looking at pictures of spiders, then watching videos, and eventually facing a live spider. By gradually exposing yourself to the fear, you may build up tolerance.

6.6.5 Try This

Developing a good attitude towards fear involves acknowledging the fear and working through it to overcome it. Here are some exercises to help you create a positive attitude towards fear:

1. Identify your fear: The first step to overcoming fear is to identify it. Write down what you're afraid of, be as specific as possible.

2. Reframe your fear: Instead of focusing on the negative aspects of your fear, try to reframe it in a positive light. For example, if you're afraid of public speaking, reframe it as an opportunity to share your knowledge and connect with others.

3. Challenge your assumptions: Sometimes our fears are based on assumptions that may not be accurate. Ask yourself if your fear is based on fact or fiction, and logically assess them by writing it.

4. Seek support: Talk to friends, family, or a therapist about your fear if it is holding you back.

6.7 Attitude to Learning

"Live as if you were to die tomorrow. Learn as if you were to live forever."
Mahatma Gandhi

*"I am always doing that which I cannot do, in order that
I may learn how to do it."*
Pablo Picasso

*"Anyone who stops learning is old, whether at twenty or eighty.
Anyone who keeps learning stays young."*
Henry Ford

*"Tell me, and I will not forget — show me and I may remember —
but involve me, and I will understand."*
old Chinese proverb

6.7.1 What is Attitude to Learning

Attitude to Learning is the approach you take to the benefits of Learning new things and continually learning throughout our lives.

Learning is the process or acquiring knowledge and skills this can be achieved through life experience or through more formal educational settings.

6.7.2 Why Attitude to Learning is Important

Learning is an essential in our life. From the day we are born we need to learn what will get the attention of our parents, we need to learn a language and need to learn to walk. We are learning all the time whether we know it or not. There is formal learning from our education systems and informal learning from our lived experiences and mentors.

The term Life Long Leaning is very apt for what we all must do in our lives. The pace of change is very fast in the world and is likely to grow exponentially in the future. In this fast-paced world we need to be able to learn and keep up with the modern essentials in society. This is what I call Essential Learning.

In addition to this Essential Learning, it is recommended that we try to learn new things often as it keeps us interested and gives us a wider perspective. Learning something new is very good for our development as it develops new neural pathways in our brains.

The Benefits of Learning Something New

1. **It can teach you something new about yourself**

   If you learn something new it will tell you if you like it or not, how to overcome the barriers to learning and teach you what is possible.

2. **It gets you out of your comfort zone**

   This is especially true if you learn something new which is not in a field you are familiar. This wakes up your brain and encourages the development of new brain pathways

3. **It can boost your confidence**

   As it will prove that you can master new things and overcome the fear of failure.

4. It will give you a new skill or new hobby

5. It will give you new perspectives

6. It can contribute to greater creativity

The *"Action for Happiness"* movement says that learning something new contributes to happiness and is one of the keys to happier living. This has been empirically proven by many recent major studies which can be access from this movement's website. https://actionforhappiness. org/10-keys/trying-out

6.7.3 Advice for Attitude to Learning

- Learning new things is good for us and expands our knowledge and improves our brains physiology. It is key to our growth and happiness.

- Frequently seek out new learning opportunities.

6.7.4 Examples

Learning a new language: It can provide several benefits, such as increasing your communication skills, improving your cognitive abilities, and enhancing your cultural understanding.

Learning a new language can open up new job opportunities, improve your travel experiences, and help you connect with people from different backgrounds.

The benefits of learning a new language go beyond just language skills. It can also boost your thinking function, multi-task, and focus. It can increase your confidence by giving you a sense of achievement. Learning a new language also exposes you to new cultures and a wider perspective.

Personal Example

I recently started taking banjo lessons and the struggle initially was very intense. My brain found it difficult to co-ordinate my left and right fingers to play the music as I had never played any musical instrument before. My brain was challenged to read the Tabular music as I had never seen this before. My ear was challenged to listen intently to hear which note was right or wrong. My memory was challenged to remember the sequence of notes and chords for the melody. However, with much practice and many mistakes some music that was recognisable was played and it was very satisfying. I know from this new learning experience that my brain was challenged and expanded and that can only be a good thing. It also gives you a unique perspective of the potential of your brain to learn many other exciting skills. This in turn reinforces the Growth Mindset approach already discussed.

6.7.5 Try This

- Challenge yourself to learn something new outside of your Comfort Zone (i.e. something you are not familiar with).

Some suggestions include:

- Learning a new language
- Cooking a new dish
- Playing a new instrument
- Learning a new sport
- Reading a new book
- Taking up a new hobby
- Learning a new computer program
- Travelling to a new place
- Taking a course or workshop
- Volunteering for a new cause

6.8 Key Take Aways regarding Attitudes to Situations

- 7 key Attitudes to Situations are analysed in detail which are essential for happiness and fulfilment and being your Best Possible Self.

- Attitude to Failure and Adversity, Failure can be seen as the First Attempt of Learning, Adversity can make us stronger, we need to be comfortable with adversity as it is part of life, Adversity can be practiced in preparation for the inevitability of it, we need to focus on what we can control

- Attitude to Opportunity, we need to act fast to seize opportunities, and be prepared and attentive to opportunities.

- Attitude to Change, we need to adapt to, enjoy and anticipate change as change is constant. We can prepare for change.

- Attitudes to Productivity, we need to be productive not just busy, when doing anything we need to ask is it essential, and does it matter i.e., is contributing to and aligned with my beliefs, values and attitudes and your Life Purpose. Bullet Journals can help considerably with productivity.

- Attitude to Communication, Elements of Personal Communication is 7% spoken words, 38% voice and tone, and 55% body language. Practice being an effective communicator by the use of active listening, being clear and concise, engaging your audience and using non verbal communication methods.

- <u>Attitude to Fear</u>, Fear can take the forms of Danger Fear, Specific Fear and Background Fear. Danger Fear is natural and is there to help protect us. Specific and Background fear can hold us back and can be overcome to help us be more productive.

- <u>Attitude to Learning</u>, Learning new things is good for us and expands our knowledge and improves our brains physiology. It is key to our growth and happiness.

CHAPTER 7

Examining Your Key Attitudes to Others

Introduction

Attitude is how you treat yourself, others and how you approach situations based on your values and beliefs.

Attitudes to Others are the attitudes in the definition above which refer to "how you treat….others". This refers to key attitudes to how we treat others which in my opinion and many other experts opinions are the best attitude to have when dealing with other people and things.

I will be describing these attitudes to Others in detail in Chapter 7. They include the following

- Attitude to Service/Contribution
- Attitude to Negotiations
- Attitude to Money
- Attitude to Letting Go
- Attitude to Relationships
- Attitude to Seeking Help

Putting these Key Attitudes to others into practice will help you greatly on your own journey to becoming your Best Possible Self.

For each Attitude to Others I will describe the following:

181

- What is the Attitude
- Why it is Important
- What advice is given for this Attitude
- Examples of this Attitude in use
- Try this yourself

7.1 Attitude to Service/Contribution

"When you cease to make a contribution, you begin to die."
Eleanor Roosevelt

"Too much of our time we spend our lives visiting the world instead of shaping It."
Oliver James Atomic Habits

"Whatever you've gained is a gift you can give back."
Ashley Ford

"Selfless service is the rent you pay for living on this wonderful planet."
Mohamad Ali

"There are many different kinds of power, true power comes from serving and helping others."
Dalai Lama

"Significance in life is in serving."
Rick Warren

"The most noble thing you can do is to give to others. Start focusing on your higher purpose."
Robin Sharma

"The quality of your life ultimately comes down to the quality of your contribution."
Robin S Sharma

"The best way to find yourself is to lose yourself in the service of others."
Mahatma Gandhi

7.1.1 What is Attitude to Service/Contribution

Attitude to Service is your approach to how you incorporate Service and Contribution in your life.

Service is defined as "action of helping or doing work for someone" - Oxford Languages. It is a form of giving. We can think of many examples of service in our lives such as volunteers who give of their time to help sporting organisations, charities and community organisations.

7.1.2 Why is Attitude to Service Important

In his Book "The Purpose Driven Life" Rick Warren poses the question to us all. How can I serve. What is in your hand? in other words what have you been given that can help others. We all have something to give from our skills, experiences both good and bad. Warren states that the purpose of influence is to speak up for those who have less influence. He poses this question to us all:

"We have been given stewardship of affluence and influence; you are responsible for what you have been given What are you doing with what you have been given?"

Dr. Martin Seligman asked two groups of students to try two activities in his book "Flourish."

Choice 1: Do something you really enjoy.

Choice 2: Do something nice/kind for someone else (Service).

Most people would guess that choice 1 would be more satisfying. But the answer was surprising.

Both groups got a momentary burst of joy doing choice 1 and 2. However the Choice 2 generated happiness that lasted all day long.

Being kind helps others, but it also helps you! I do not advocate to be kind because it helps you but it is a nice by-product of kindness. It a classic win/win situation, the other person benefits (win) and you benefit (win).

The *"Action for Happiness"* movement says that helping others contributes considerably to happiness and is one of the keys to happier living. This has been empirically proven by many recent major studies which can be access from this movement's website.

https://www.actionforhappiness.org/10-keys-to-happier-living/do-things-for-others/details

In their book "The Go Giver" Burg and Mann introduce the notion of the Go Giver. This is a person who focuses on adding value and giving.

Go Getters are different as they can take action and get things done but generally focus on what they can gain. Go Givers on the other hand can do the same but they can give and serve and add value. They think in terms of what they can give to others and, according to the authors, are often more successful than Go Getters. It works on the idea that what is given eventually comes back around if the person is open to receiving it. Their value is often determined by the number of people they can serve as opposed to how much they own. Many example of how this works in real life and business are given in the book.

7.1.3 Advice for Attitude to Service

- Service is a key to our happiness, it is a win/win situation where you benefit and others benefit.

- We need to incorporate as many acts of service into our lives as possible as it is a truly human thing to do for others.

- We need to ask the question "what is in our hands" that we can give back to others. We all have something to give from our skills, experiences both good and bad.

- True power comes from Service "There are many different kinds of power, true power comes from serving and helping others" – Dalai Lama.

7.1.4 Personal Examples

These moments of giving back for me have been some of the most satisfying and fulfilling parts of my life and I know if you decide to give back, they will be for you too. Below are some of my own examples of service in action.

I recall the great feelings I received from being involved in something greater than myself on a voluntary basis. I was in the 72nd Cub Scouts and Scouts in Raheny Dublin for many years from the age of 6 to my early 20s. I really enjoyed all the adventure over those years and it was great to give back to Scouting by being a Troop Leader for many years and Leader of the 72nd Adventure Scouts Group for many years also. I know I received valuable leadership experience which was of great benefit to me in my many professional and voluntary roles thereafter.

My passion for Hillwalking also motivated me to setup a Hillwalking Club in Dublin called the Marley Hillwalkers in 1993. The Club started when I approached a small group of walkers in Marley Park in Rathfarnham in Dublin and asked them if they would like to explore some more challenging walks. I was a qualified Mountain Leader at that stage so I felt confident about leading the way. As Rick Warren puts it this qualification was "in my hand" and I was ready to serve. The walkers loved the extra challenge and beauty of the Wicklow mountains. So much was their enthusiasm for the hills they went on to organise many international trips including a trip to the Himalayas. That Club is still going from strength to strength today with over 100 members currently. I feel very proud to have been even a small part of this Club and its activities in its formative years. I got so much pleasure from the fun, relationships and friendship formed than any of the inputs I made. This was a clear indication to me of the power of Service/Contribution.

Following a long career in education at all levels I also came to the realisation that I had something else "in my hand" to give back from this experience. I had accumulated 30 years of experience with dealing with both staff and young peoples' issues. I decided to volunteer for a national organisation which provides free 24 hour Listening Service and Emotional Support. This requires only a small commitment of a few hours each week. I have been volunteering for this service for the past 16 years. This has given me a whole new perspective on life and what others have to deal with in their lives and I feel privileged and honoured to be of any help to those in a crisis. You feel you have something to offer and in the words of the Dalai Lama it is a powerful feeling "true power comes from serving and helping others." Again this experience has given me more than I have given and is another example of a win/win situation.

I have a lifelong friend, Tommy Campbell, for the past 40 years. He is a real inspiration to me and many people by how he has dealt with his challenges. He is totally blind since he was 3½ years of age. He loved hillwalking and outdoor sports when he was younger and this is where I met him on an An Oige cycle 40 years ago. I admired his motivation and persistence on that cycle. He loved to go cycling on his tandem and had some sighted pilots to help him. He asked if I would like to be a pilot as he was finding it difficult to get sighted pilots at that time. I was delighted to help. For 20 years after that we went on many cycles on his Dawes tandems. We started with small day cycles to Howth and different areas around Dublin. We later went on weekend cycles to Wicklow. We even went abroad on cycling holidays. We completed Scotland Coast to Coast on the tandem and England Coast to Coast. We cycled around the hilly Cotswolds region in England and also cycled the entire Hook of Holland on that tandem. We are still friends to this day and I feel I am privileged to have his friendship for so long.

7.1.5 Try This

- Consider what is in your hand that you can give back to others who could benefit from this and take ACTION to SERVE others.

- Challenge yourself to engaging in acts of kindness/service. Choose an idea from the list below or create your own.

  - Write a "Thank You" card.
  - Send a text congratulating/complimenting or praising someone.
  - Write a letter to your parents/friends/neighbours expressing your gratitude to them.
  - Call one of you family at random.
  - Help a blind person or old person across the road.
  - Donate Blood.
  - Become a Mentor.
  - Volunteer.
  - Open the Door for somebody.
  - Donate money to a person, cause or charity.

7.2 Attitude to Negotiations

*"If there is negotiation, it must be rooted in mutual respect
and concern for the rights of others."*
John F. Kennedy

*"The true test of the success of a negotiation is the results of the relationship
formed as a result of the negotiation."*
William Fosdick Morrison

7.2.1 What is Attitude to Negotiations

Attitude to negotiation is your approach to how you interact/negotiate with others.
Negotiations are discussions aimed at reaching an agreement.

7.2.2 Why is Attitude to Negotiations Important

We are always negotiating in our lives both personally and in business or professionally.
Personally, we negotiate when we get married or are in a relationship, we have to agree or comprise all the time.
In business we are constantly negotiating deals.

Covey in his book "The 7 Habits of Highly Effective People" says the best situation is where both sides win if possible. This is called a "Win/Win" situation. It is an attitude toward life that seeks mutual benefit for all parties where possible. For example, you are selling a car and give a large discount (win for customer) but also you are making a profit (win for the seller).

Covey also says most people think "Win/Lose" where all they are interested about is themselves and their success often at the expense of the other. Its underlining assumption is scarcity thinking, a belief there is not enough for everybody so you have to get what you want at other people's expense. It means winning is beating somebody else. It is based on the competitive approach and not the cooperative approach.

Another approach is the "Lose/Win" approach. This is where you are a people pleaser. You avoid confrontation and let other people win at your expense.

Another approach is the "Lose/Lose" approach. This is where both parties lose. This is often blinded by hatred where you want to harm others even if it is at your own expense. Example a judge in a divorce case says all assets must be shared when sold on a 50/50 basis. The husband sells his car valued at €10000 for €1000 so that his wife only gets 500 euro.

"Win" this is where what the other person gets is irrelevant as long as I win. This is a common approach to negotiations. The approach ignores the other parties needs/wants and becomes a missed opportunity for good relationships.

Key components for developing environments that encourage Win/Win relationships in Business are

1. You need to develop integrity, maturity and an abundance mentality.

2. You must develop relationships with high-emotional bank accounts where trust is built up over time.

3. You must have agreed results, guidelines, support and accountability.

4. Systems in business need to be developed to support win/win setups.

5. Processes need to be agreed which include seeing the problem from the other point of view, identifying key issues, what a solution looks like and identifying possible new options.

7.2.3 Advice for Attitude to Negotiations

- Try to think Win/Win in any negotiation situation. It is an attitude toward life that seeks mutual benefit for all parties where possible.

7.2.4 Examples

Win/win situations are those where both parties involved benefit from the outcome. Here are some examples:

Negotiating a raise at work: If an employee approaches their employer with a request for a raise, a win/win outcome can be achieved if the employer agrees to the raise and the employee agrees to some increase in productivity. The employee benefits from the increased salary, while the employer benefits from the employee's increased productivity.

Sharing resources: Such as equipment or space, both parties benefit. For example, a gym may allow a personal trainer to use their facility to train clients for free, and in return, the personal trainer may recommend the gym to their clients.

Resolving a conflict: In a conflict situation a win/win outcome can be achieved through effective communication and compromise. For example, two neighbours may have a dispute over a property line, but a win/win outcome can be achieved if they work together to come up with a mutually beneficial solution.

7.2.5 Try This

Win/win skills refer to the ability to collaborate and work towards mutually beneficial outcomes, rather than approaching a situation with a competitive approach or one-upmanship. Here is one exercise that can help improve win/win skills:

Role-playing exercises: Practice different scenarios where you and another person have different interests or goals, and try to find a solution that benefits both parties. This could be as simple as deciding where to go for lunch or what to watch on television with a colleague or agreeing the price to pay for something or resolving a conflict.

7.3 Attitude to Money

"Wealth consists not in having great possessions but in having few wants"
Epictetus

"Many folks think they aren't good at earning money when what they don't know is how to use it."
Frank A. Clark

7.3.1 What is Attitude to Money

Attitude to Money is your approach to how you spend and save money as a resource.

7.3.2 Why Attitude to Money is important

There are millions of pages written about what to do with money and how to make it. However, the simplest model I have come across, years ago, is that given by Jim Rohn the motivational speaker and multi-millionaire. He gives very simple financial advice to children in schools and colleges. He illustrates his thinking by using the theme "what to do with a dollar" in his book "The Keys to Success" (2013).

He starts by explaining that if a child or teenager is gifted or earns a dollar what should he/she do with it? Most children will say they will spend all of it. But Rohn advises otherwise. He points out that those who spend it all consistently will not generate wealth and may even be poor.

He advises the following strategy for the dollar:

ONE DOLLAR-HOW TO SPEND IT

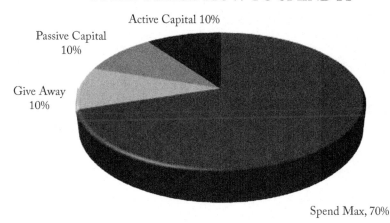

Active Capital 10%

Passive Capital
10%

Give Away
10%

Spend Max, 70%

Spend up to a maximum of 70%

Give 10% away to worthy causes or other worthy projects. This teaches
generosity and encourages thinking of others less fortunate or in need.
Make sure you understand what the money is being used for. He goes
on to say you should ask for a tour of the charity or cause to understand
what the money is used for no matter how small the donation.

Set aside 10% to Passive Capital. He explains his simple
description of capital as any value you set aside to be invested in any
enterprise that brings value to the market place hoping to make a
profit. Passive capital is described as making your money work for you
by investing it so that it gives a return. This might be lodging your
money in a bank and earning compound interest or investing in stocks
or prize bonds etc. This return should be re-invested into a fund for
further investment.

The final 10% should be set aside to Active Capital This is where you engage in some activity to make a profit. For children this could be buying an old bicycle and fixing it up and adding value to it and selling it for a profit. This profit should be re-invested into this profit fund for further projects.

Rohn advocates that this practice should start early and it will prove to be successful in the long run if the approach is practiced consistently. He says that this should be taught in schools and he wishes he was taught this early in his career as this approach when taught to him made him millions. He also states that he lost millions but the real thing he valued was what he became as a person. He managed to earn back his millions very quickly once he used what he learned along the way. He also suggests that the rich invest first then spend and the poor spend first and invest what's left over which is often not a lot.

7.3.3 Advice for Attitude to Money

- Jim Rohan's advice maybe a useful approach to consider when spending or saving money effectively. as it considers others. However there are many other approach you could take. Consider the 70%,10%,10%,10% rule.

7.3.4 Examples

See examples above.

7.3.5 Try This

- Try Jim Rohan's methods of spending money on a small amount of money for a period of 6 months and evaluate the benefits of this approach.

- If this approach works for you consider using the approach further.

7.4 Attitude to Letting Go/Forgiveness

"If you let go a little, you will have a little peace, if you let go a lot, you will have a lot of peace, if you let go completely, you will have complete peace."
Ajahn Chah

"To be wronged is nothing, unless you continue to remember it."
Confucius

"Resentment is like drinking poison and then hoping it will kill your enemies."
Nelson Mandela

"The weak can never forgive. Forgiveness is the attribute of the strong."
Mahatma Gandhi

"Forgiveness is not an occasional act; it is a constant attitude."
Martin Luther King Jr.

"Forgiveness is a gift you give yourself."
Tony Robbins

7.4.1 What is Attitude to Letting Go

Attitude to Letting Go is your approach to Letting go of emotions, things and acts of forgiveness that are of benefit to you and others.

Letting Go is defined as to stop holding something or to stop thinking about or being angry about the past or something that happened in the past.

7.4.2 Why Attitude to Letting Go is Important

Having the right attitude towards letting go is important for several reasons:

1. Reduces stress: Holding on to things that no longer serve us can create stress and anxiety. When we let go of these things, we free ourselves from their emotional pull and create more mental space and peace.

2. Promotes personal growth: Letting go of old beliefs, habits, and relationships can allow us to grow and evolve as individuals. We become more open to new experiences and opportunities that can lead to personal growth and development.

3. Improves relationships: Letting go of grudges and resentments can improve our relationships with others. We become more forgiving, compassionate, and understanding, which can lead to stronger and more meaningful connections with others.

4. Enhances creativity: Letting go of old ideas and ways of doing things can open up space for new and innovative ideas to emerge. We become more creative and innovative in our thinking and problem-solving.

7.4.3 Advice for Attitude to Letting Go

- Letting go can be our doorway to freedom, practice letting go emotions and things.

- Forgiveness is the attitude of the strong and it is a gift you give yourself and should be practiced whenever appropriate.

7.4.4 Examples

Letting Go - Emotions

Some thoughts and emotions we hold on to as positive memories. Other thoughts we generally push away and avoid, these are usually uncomfortable or frightening thoughts, however they are also stored in our minds often with high levels of emotional intensity. Jon Kabat Zinn, an expert in Mindfulness, says that we should try to experience them as they are, without getting caught up in them by neither pushing thoughts or emotions away nor holding on to them.

Jon Kabat-Zinn uses an analogy of how monkeys are hunted. Monkey catchers use certain methods to catch monkeys. One method is to hang a coconut on a tree with a small hole bored out to allow the monkey to put its hand in. To attract the monkeys to the coconut they put a banana inside. The monkey is attracted to the scent of the banana and will put its hand in to the hole to grasp the banana. It cannot get its hand out when it is holding the banana. The Monkey will stay there holding on not realising it could let the banana go by releasing its hand.

Jon compares us to the monkey where we are holding on to certain thoughts and emotions but we have the ability to let them go to be as they are. When you are caught by your own desire or by your own attachment to things being a certain way that's painful and letting go is your "doorway to freedom". And it is something that you can practice every time you catch yourself clinging to something, you remind yourself to release it and let it be and let it go. The breath can remind us of this natural process... every time we take a breath in, we have to release it out to allow another breath in.

If we store past difficult issues and emotions these can be stored in what Eckhart Tolle, author, calls the Pain Body. These are painful issues which have been stored and some trigger will suddenly bring these thoughts to the fore and take over your mind and emotions again. At this point these painful emotions are played out again. Tolle says it is better to have let these thoughts and emotions go so that they do not get a chance to be relived over and over again.

Letting Go - Things

Another take on letting go is coming from minimalists. Minimalism is defined as the process of identifying what is essential in your life and having the courage to let go of the rest. It often starts with decluttering your home and examining what possessions are essential. It also involves questioning unexamined consumerism.

The authors Millburn and Nicodemus in their book "Minimalism" outline in detail how to live the Minimalist Life. In the book, they explain how anyone can make small daily changes to achieve a clutter-free, debt-free, and fulfilling life and this can then allow one to focus on, what they deem are five key areas: health, relationships, passions, growth, and contributing to others.

Both authors had lived the American dream of corporate and material success but it left them unhappy, exhausted, and deeply in debt. Following the death of one of the authors mothers he was faced with the challenge of clearing all his mothers' possessions. This led him to question his own life and all the material "stuff" he had accumulated. They both quit their jobs, re-examined their lives, and started the popular website TheMinimalists.com which has many excellent resources on how to let go of unnecessary stuff and excessive consumerism in order to have more time for some of the more important things in life.

Letting Go - Forgiveness

Forgiveness is another form of letting go. It is about giving mercy to those who have harmed us in some way. It is not about condoning or accepting the offender and letting them off. But according to the author Roberto Ensight's book "8 Keys to Forgiveness" 2015 it is well worth the effort to forgive.

Forgiveness can heal and allow us to move on in life. According to the author studies have shown that it can decrease depression, anxiety, unhealthy anger and some symptoms of Post-Traumatic Stress Disorder.

Forgiveness is a two-way process it can not only help you but also extend to the other person.

The author urges us to practice forgiving and empathy whenever we can for the small things so that we are "forgivingly fit" and empathetic for the bigger challenges.

The author stresses the importance of finding meaning in suffering not to diminish the pain but to find meaning such as new perspectives, finding your resilience and strengthening your inner resolve.

We tend to be very harsh and unforgiving to ourselves and again the author urges self-compassion and forgiveness.

The author reminds us all that the more hurt incurred the more important forgiveness is. However, this can be very challenging and may need the help of a professional to support this process.

7.4.5 Try This

Letting go can be a difficult but necessary process for personal growth and well-being. Here is an exercise you can try to help you let go of negative emotions or experiences:

1. Visualize a situation or emotion that you want to let go of. It could be a past mistake, a grudge, a trauma or a negative thought.

2. As you visualize the situation, try to observe it without judgment or attachment.

3. Imagine yourself holding a balloon or a piece of paper. Write down the situation or emotion on the paper or visualize it inside the balloon.

4. Release the balloon or the paper and watch it float away.

5. As you let go of the balloon or the paper, repeat an affirmation, such as "I am letting go of this thing or situation" or "I am free from negative emotions."

6. Take a few minutes to sit with the feeling of release and relief.

This exercise may need to be repeated multiple times to feel the full effect. It can also be helpful to talk to a therapist or trusted friend or family member.

7.5 Attitude to Relationships

"The good life is built with good relationships."
Mark Twain

"Good relationships are not made in a day; good relationships are made daily."
Dr. Abby Medcalf

"Communication to a relationship is like oxygen is to life,
without it, it dies."
Tony A. Gaskins Jr.

"Close relationships make the good times better and the
difficult times easier."
Adam Jackson

"In a genuine relationship, there is an outward flow of open, alert
attention towards the other person in which there is no wanting
whatsoever. That alert attention is Presence. It is the prerequisite for any
authentic relationship."
Eckhart Tolle

7.5.1 What is Attitude to Relationships

Attitude to Relationships is our approach to relationships which are beneficial to our happiness and fulfilment.

"Relationships are the way in which two or more people are connected...
and behave towards each other."
Oxford Languages

7.5.2 Why our Attitude to Relationships is important

We all need and form relationships in our daily lives with families, our friends and our work colleagues and our customers and communities.

These social connections are really good for us and are essential for our daily existence. Good relationships have been proven to keep us happier and healthier.

One of the longest studies on happiness was conducted over a period of 75 years where the participants were tracked for this period. This was conducted by The Harvard Study of Adult Development Project (www.adultdevelopmentstudy.org). Its current Director is Robert Waldinger

Since 1938, they tracked the lives of two groups of men. The first group started in the study when they were undergraduates at Harvard College. They all finished college during World War II, and then most went off to serve in the war.

And the second group that they followed was a group of boys from Boston's poorest neighbourhoods, boys who were chosen for the study specifically because they were from some of the most troubled and disadvantaged families in the Boston Area of the 1930s. Most lived in tenements, many without hot and cold running water.

The key lesson from the study was: good relationships keep us happier and healthier.

Three big lessons about relationships emerged from the Study:

1. Social connections are really good for us, and that loneliness kills. People who are more socially connected to family, to friends, to community, are happier.

2. The quality of your close relationships is what really matters.

3. Good relationships don't just protect our bodies, they protect our brains.

The study stated:

"Just like the millennials in that recent survey, many of our men when they were starting out as young adults really believed that fame and wealth and high achievement were what they needed to go after to have a good life. But over and over, over these 75 years, our study has shown that the people who fared the best were the people who leaned in to relationships, with family, with friends, with community."

What might leaning in to relationships look like? It might include

- replacing screen time with people time

- livening up a stale relationship by doing something new together

- reaching out to a family or friend who you haven't spoken to in years etc.

The "Action for Happiness" movement says that People with strong and broad social relationships are happier and is one of the movement's 10 keys to Happiness. This has been empirically proven by many major studies which can be access from this movement's website. https://www.actionforhappiness.org/10-keys-to-happier-living/connect-with-people/details

Eckhart Tolle in his book "Oneness with all Life" (this book is a collection of inspirational selections from his book New Earth) says that when we meet with people in work or other circumstances, we should give them our fullest attention. He says you should make this the primary purpose of your interaction with them to enable quality attention and consciousness to flow into the interaction. The secondary purpose is the reason for the interaction. For example...

I have a meeting with a person to possibly sell them something.

- Primary Purpose = Fill my awareness of the person I am meeting and give them my full attention, thinking of myself is not important.

- Secondary Purpose = Sales talk possibly leading to a sale.

Emotional Responsiveness (ER)is key to great relationships. 3 Key components of ER according to – Dr. Abby Medcalf

- Accessible: are you available when needed
- Responsiveness: can you celebrate good times and care in bad times
- Engagement is your number 1 priority

Typical ER blocks are

- Believing that partners are adults and do not need ER
- Stress
- Disconnected with your own needs and feelings and hence disregard others feelings

What we can do about the blocks to ER

1. Commit to be an ER partner
2. Destress to be more available
3. If your parents were very invasive or very unresponsive you may have to seek some external help
4. Start to notice your own emotions so that you can notice others

7.5.3 Advice for Attitude to Relationships

- The quality of our key relationships are critical to our health and happiness
- We should lean in our relationships
- We should all recognise the qualities of healthy, unhealthy and abusive relationships and try to foster healthy relationships where possible (see the following examples)

- Emotional responsiveness is key to great relationships.

- To improve human interactions make your primary purpose your full awareness and attention to the person.

7.5.4 Examples

Relationships Exist on a Spectrum

It is important that our attitude to relationships is formed with the knowledge of what constitutes a healthy, unhealthy and an abusive relationship. According to HEALTHY RELATIONSHIP HIGH SCHOOL EDUCATORS' TOOLKIT from Loveisrespect.org and other sources some the following are the key attributes of these types of relationships.

A healthy relationship means that you are:

- Communicating: You talk openly about problems, listen to each other and respect each other's opinions.

- Respectful: You value each other as you are. You respect each other's emotional, digital and sexual boundaries.

- Trusting: You believe what your partner has to say. You do not feel the need to "prove" each other's trustworthiness.

- Honest: You are honest with each other, but can still keep some things private.

- Equal: You make decisions together and hold each other to the same standards. Also there is equal proportion of give and take where power is shared.

- Enjoying personal time: You both can enjoy spending time apart, alone or with others. You respect each other's need for time apart.

- Each person helps the other to develop and grow.

- Conflicts are dealt with quickly and ill feeling is not let fester.

You may be in an unhealthy relationship if one or both partners is:

- Not communicating: When problems arise, you fight or you don't discuss them at all.

- Disrespectful: One or both partners are not considerate of the other's feelings and/or personal boundaries.

- Not trusting: One partner doesn't believe what the other says, or feels entitled to invade their privacy.

- Dishonest: One or both partners tell lies.

- Trying to take control: One partner feels their desires and choices are more important.

- Only spending time with your partner: Your partner's community is the only one you socialize in.

- Conflicts are let remain unresolved

- Unequal giving and taking in the relationship.

Abuse is occurring in a relationship when one partner:

- Communicates in a way that is hurtful, threatening, insulting or demeaning.

- Disrespects the feelings, thoughts, decisions, opinions or physical safety of the other. Physically hurts or injures the other partner by hitting, slapping, choking, pushing, shoving or shouting.

- Blames the other partner for their harmful actions, makes excuses for abusive actions and/or minimizes the abusive behaviour.

- Controls and isolates the other partner by telling them what to wear, who they can hang out with, where they can go and/or what they can do.

- Pressures or forces the other partner to do things they don't want to do; threatens, hurts or blackmails their partner if they resist or say no

7.5.5 Try This

Consider a relationship you are in or was in and consider whether it is or was

- A Healthy Relationship
- Or An Unhealthy Relationship
- Or An Abusive Relationship

Using the Attributes listed in the Examples given in 7.5.4 above.

7.6 Attitude to Seeking Help

"Don't be afraid to ask questions. Don't be afraid to ask for help when you need it. I do that every day. Asking for help isn't a sign of weakness, it's a sign of strength. It shows you have the courage to admit when you don't know...."
Barrack Obama

"Most people don't get those experiences because they never ask. I never found anybody that didn't want to help me if I asked them for help."
Steve Jobs Apple Inc. founder

"When we have done our very, very best, papa, and that is not enough, then I think the right time must have come for asking help of others." -
Charles Dickens

7.6.1 What is an Attitude to Seeking Help

An Attitude to Seeking Help is an approach to seeking help when needed and not being reluctant to seek it in the first place.

Seeking Help means to go in search of advice, help or assistance when it is needed. It includes

1. Becoming aware of symptoms and making a judgement that assistance may be required.

2. Expressing the symptoms /issues that they are experiencing and may need some support.

3. The person should be made aware of the sources of help available to assist.

7.6.2 Why Attitude to Seeking Help is Important

Seeking help from others is a sign of strength. Man is not an island. We often need the help of others but we frequently are reluctant to ask for it. It is sometimes seen as a sign of weakness but we should heed the advice of Barrack Obama in the quote where he states that asking for help is *"a sign of strength"*

When we see "self-made" individuals we often do not see all the help they have got from behind the scenes. Often those who are asked for help are delighted to be asked and will be more likely to help again. Asking for help is seen by the person who is asked for help as "a subtle but effective form of flattery" and they will more likely help you again. This phenomenon is known as the "Ben Franklin Effect."

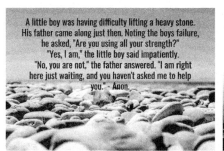

A little boy was having difficulty lifting a heavy stone. His father came along just then. Noting the boys failure, he asked, "Are you using all your strength?" "Yes, I am," the little boy said impatiently. "No, you are not," the father answered. "I am right here just waiting, and you haven't asked me to help you." - Anon.

The healthy and strong individual is the one who asks for help when he needs it.
Rona Barrett

7.6.3 Advice for Attitude to Seeking Help

- The strong individual is the one who asks for help when he needs it.

- Seek out help in its many forms such as mentorship, family, friend colleague help, professional advice, national organisation help and advice and many other sources (see examples below).

- Seek accountability and feedback from others when seeking help.

7.6.4 Examples

Seeking help can take on many forms:

Mentorship. Learning from someone who has more experience or skill and knows what does and doesn't work can really help your development and speed up the time required to learn essential information and skills.

Seek out a friend/family member or colleague or therapist to work on any mental health issues. Just having a confidential listener can do wonders for your healing this could be from a friend or family or a trusted colleague.

If you've been unsuccessfully trying to work through any mental health issues such as trauma or experiences, seek help from a professional /therapist.

Many studies have been done into the key barriers to help seeking. A detailed literature review was published in 2010 by Gulliver et al. which reviewed 15 qualitative and 7 quantitative studies of young people's experiences of help-seeking for mental health issues. Key themes in the barriers young people identified to help-seeking were:

- Stigma and embarrassment
- Problems recognising symptoms
- Preference for self-reliance
- Confidentiality and trust
- Hopelessness

Seek the help of National Helplines and Organisations and websites which can provide help and support. One of the best lists I have seen in Ireland of such National Helplines and Organisations can be accessed at https://about.rte.ie/ie/helplines This list gives a comprehensive list of contact information and advice and websites for all the helplines and support agencies in Ireland. It is given under the following headings:

- Abuse Domestic Violence
- Addiction
- Alzheimer's and Dementia
- Asylum Seekers Support
- Autism
- Bereavement
- Bullying
- Crisis Pregnancy
- Depression
- Eating Disorders
- Financial Advice
- Health
- Homelessness
- LGBT Support
- Mental Health
- Miscarriage Support
- Online Safety
- Parenting Support
- Racism
- Sexual Abuse
- Suicide and Self-Harm
- Support in General
- Youth Mental Health

Get a friend/family member/colleague to keep you on track for a goal. A goal will be more likely achieved if you share it with somebody else. You will be accountable not only to yourself but somebody else.

Join a Toastmasters or Drama Group to get feedback on your speaking and presentation skills. Get on stage and have more experienced people guide you. These groups are literally designed to give clear, honest feedback and support. This will develop your wit, sense of humour, help with overcoming any social anxiety.

7.6.5 Try This

Exercise on Seeking Help:

1. Identify an area in your life where you could use some help. It could be anything from work issues to personal issues. Write it down.

2. List the people in your life who could possibly provide you with help in the area you identified in 1. above. It could be a work colleague, a family member, a friend or a professional. Write down their names.

3. Choose one person from the list in 2. above.

4. Think about what you would say to this person to ask for their help. Write it down and be specific about what you need help with and how you think they could assist you.

5. Make a plan to contact this person. Take action and ask for the help you need. Remember, seeking help is a sign of strength, not weakness.

7.7 Key Take Aways regarding Attitudes to Others

6 key Attitudes to Others and Things are analysed in detail which are essential for happiness and fulfilment and being your Best Possible Self.

- <u>Attitude to Service/Contribution</u>, Service is a key to happiness, it is a win/win situation where you benefit and others benefit. Seek out as many occasions where you can be of Service.

- <u>Attitude to Negotiations</u>, think win/win where possible.

- <u>Attitude to Money</u> consider the 70%,10%,10%,10% rule

- <u>Attitude to Letting Go/Forgiveness</u>, Letting go can be our doorway to freedom, practice letting go emotions and things. Forgiveness is the attitude of the strong and it is a gift you give yourself

- <u>Attitude to Relationship</u>, the quality of our key Relationships is critical to our health and happiness, we should lean into our relationships, we should all recognise the qualities of healthy, unhealthy and abusive relationships. Emotional responsiveness is key to great relationships.

- <u>Attitude to Seeking Help</u>, the strong individual is the one who asks for help when he needs it, seeking help takes many forms such as mentorship, seeking help with mental help issues, Accountability and Feedback.

CHAPTER 8

BECOMING YOUR BEST
POSSIBLE SELF

Introduction

"Think of the fierce energy concentration in an Acorn, you bury it in the ground and it expands into an Oak!"
George Bernard Shaw

"Unless you want to have a life that is directed by others and boxes you in, you need to decide for yourself what to do and you need to have the courage to do it."
Ray Dalio

Taking all that was said in the previous chapters we will now look at the table again that was presented in the introduction. The transition from Old Self to a Best Possible Self can be explained by being aware of what personal transformation is and how it relates to the model.

We will discuss the transition for Old Self to new Best Possible Self-based from the table based on all the knowledge presented in the previous chapters.

Old Self

The Old Self could be considered as the person farthest away from becoming your Best Possible Self.

The old self-identity is based on the ego which creates our identity from our life experience and beliefs. This can be a positive identity but is often negative based on the egos belief that we are conditionally accepted based on certain conditions being met, such as achieving and having certain things. For the old self attachment to achievement and things are very important as it forms part of the identity. Old self's self-esteem is based on the external things being achieved or owned. If these are taken away identity is lost and this can create fear and often the view is that everything is good outside of the oneself. However, based on this external focus we are striving for and get externals but it is never enough. To the old self success is often seen as a certain destination, when I achieve my goals, I then will be happy. However often when the goal is achieved there is something else to be achieved and on and on goes the process of striving. The old self is constantly searching for meaning and completeness... questions arise such as... is there is something missing? am I whole? Am I good enough? etc.

Often the old self is focused on the past and future and often disregards the present. Analysing and comparing with others occupies a lot of your thoughts. The mind identity often is very full with all these thoughts and often works on auto pilot to carry out tasks. This focus disconnects you from the present and hence current moments are often missed. The ego identified self is often very critical of self and practices negative self-talk often.

The old self often has a fixed mindset where it is very fixed in its thoughts and ego-identified view of self. The old self has a fixed mindset which is not flexible to change and can't adapt to change and different circumstances. Adversity and difficulties are often seen as devastating and demoralising.

The old self often has not spent time examining its positive beliefs and limiting beliefs and unexamined beliefs can be damaging. As most of our actions are based on our 3 key filters beliefs, values and attitudes if these are not examined in detail and aligned with our actions, we are unlikely to be happy and successful.

Taking and unappreciation is common for the Old Self. The focus is on the self and taking what you can get and not being concerned with other people. This can lead to Win/lose relationships and gratitude is not expressed.

The Best Possible Self

The Best Possible Self is seen as better as your identity is unconditionally accepted, warts and all, and is based on "being" as most important and subsequently doing and having. It is based on being the best version of yourself which is ever learning and improving where possible. When focused on being the focus is internal. Your beliefs, your values and your key attitudes become very important. Your focus is internal and the external things become less important and non-attachment is practiced. Our self-esteem is based not on external things but on our internal set of beliefs and values and attitudes. These beliefs are empowering and serve our better selves and others. Our values are well thought out and have been examined and are used to guide our actions and decisions. Our values are aligned with our actions.

Success is the quality of the moments of the journey and the person I am becoming. Success is enough. The Best Possible Self stops searching and experiences wholeness and ease through being true to oneself and its soul through its passions, inspirations and intuition. True power comes when your personality comes to serve the energy and purpose of your soul. It practises self-acceptance and does not compare itself to others only to itself. It mainly practices positive self-talk and has strategies to offset automatic negative thoughts.

The Best Possible Self examines key attitudes to ensure one can work to become the person we want to be. You live in the present most of time where you are mindful and engaged in the moment often involving many of your senses. This present focus gives you a greater awareness of your life and a keen sense of gratitude for what you already have. The quality of the present moments of your life are key to your happiness. You do not often drift into auto pilot as this state is not mindful. You stay in the present by being mindful and practicing mediation and focusing on the senses and moments. Success and happiness are based on the quality of the moments on the journey of life.

The Best Possible Self is more positive and practices positive self-talk. It focuses its thoughts not on comparing with others but with comparing one self's progress. How am I personally developing over time is the key question and the answer to that is a key barometer of progress where possible.

The Best Possible Self has a Growth Mindset which is flexible to and can change and adapt to change and different circumstances. It does not have a fixed identity. Adversity and difficulties are approached with a different frame of mind and can be turned into key learning opportunities.

The Best Possible Self often spends time examining its positive beliefs and limiting beliefs. As most of our actions are based on our 3 key filters beliefs, values and attitudes and thus these are examined in detail and aligned with our actions and goals making us more likely to be happy and successful.

The Best Possible Self is free to be creative as it can focus on its true self through its passions, inspirations and intuition which are liberating and allow creativity to blossom.

Giving and Gratitude are common for the Best Possible Self. The focus is on the internal self and service and contribution to others is common. Win/win relationships are sought and Gratitude is expressed and felt for what one is and has.

When you are striving to be your Best Possible Self you are more likely to be happy based on the empirically evidence presented.

A summary of the transition is presented again in the table below. This time I will refer to the section in the book where the Best Possible Self transition is discussed and explained.

The Transition from Old Self to Best Possible Self

Old Self	⟶	Best Possible Self
Conditional acceptance of self	⟶	Unconditional acceptance of self (see 2.4.1)
Doing /Having	⟶	Being/Doing/Having (see Introduction)
Living	⟶	Living/Enlightenment/ Awakening (see 5.2)
External Focus	⟶	Internal Focus (see Introduction)
Everything good outside	⟶	Everything good inside initially (see Introduction)
Learned Self	⟶	Original Self (see 2.4.1)
Mind Full	⟶	Mindfulness (see 5.2)
Am I Whole?	⟶	I am Whole/Self-Acceptance (see Introduction)
False Self	⟶	Real Self/true self (see Chapter 2)
Lower level of Consciousness	⟶	Higher level of Consciousness (see 5.2)
Fearful self	⟶	Loving self

Critical self	⟶	Non-Critical/ Affirmative Self (see 5.1)
EGO	⟶	Soul /Spirit
Searching for Wholeness	⟶	Experiences Wholeness
Body/Mind	⟶	Body/Mind/Soul/Spirit
Dreams	⟶	Dreams/Awakens
Auto Pilot	⟶	Fully Conscious/Aware/ Mindful
Analysing	⟶	Sensing
Avoidance of Difficult Emotions	⟶	Approaching difficult emotions (see 6.1 and 7.4)
Depleting Energy	⟶	Nourishing
Not living by Values	⟶	Living by Values (see Chapter 3)
Unexamined Attitudes	⟶	Examined Attitudes (see Chapters 4-7)
Unexamined Beliefs	⟶	Examined Beliefs (see Chapter 2)
Unappreciative	⟶	Gratitude (see 5.4)
Comparing with Others	⟶	Self-Acceptance / Personal Growth/ Comparing with past Self
Striving	⟶	Accepting/Ease
Attachment	⟶	Non attachment (see 7.4)
Uncreative self	⟶	Creative Self (see 5.5)
Reactive self	⟶	Non-reactive/ Proactive self (see 6.4)
Taking	⟶	Giving (see 7.1)
I am not good enough	⟶	I am good enough (see Chapter 2)

Powerless	→	Powerful/Responsible/ Proactive (see 6.4)
No Goals	→	Goals Set in line with values and beliefs (see Chapter 3 and 5.3)
Fixed Mindset	→	Growth Mindset (see Chapter 4)
Adversity	→	Growth (see Chapter 4)
Change	→	Opportunity (see 6.2)
Thinking	→	Awareness (see 5.2)
Win/ Lose	→	Win/Win (see 7.2)
Past and Future Focus	→	Present Focus (see 5.2)
Unexamined Daily Habits	→	Examined and Empowering Daily Habits (see 5.7)
Success is a destination	→	Success is the quality of the moments of the journey (see 5.2)
Success is never enough	→	Success is enough (see 5.2)

Try This

- As an exercise to consolidate your knowledge of the transition to your Best Possible Self, try filling in the form in Appendix 2.

- Then use the completed form as a guide during your transition phase.

Key Take Away in this Chapter

The transition from the Old Self to the Best Possible Self is outlined.

The Old Self has many of the following traits:

- Conditional acceptance of self
- Doing /Having
- Living
- External Focus
- Everything good outside
- Learned Self
- Mind Full
- Am I Whole?
- False Self
- Lower level of Consciousness
- Fearful self
- Critical self
- EGO
- Searching for Wholeness
- Body/Mind
- Dreams
- Auto Pilot
- Analysing
- Avoidance of Difficult Emotions
- Depleting Energy
- Not living by Values
- Unexamined Attitudes
- Unexamined Beliefs
- Unappreciative
- Comparing with Others

- Striving
- Attachment
- Uncreative self
- Reactive self
- Taking
- I am not good enough
- Powerless
- No Goals
- Fixed Mindset
- Adversity
- Thinking
- Win/ Lose
- Past and Future Focus
- Unexamined Daily Habits
- Success is a destination
- Success is never enough

The Best Possible Self will have as many of the following traits. All of these traits have been explained in detail in the book.

- Unconditional acceptance of self
- Being/Doing/Having
- Living/Enlightenment/ Awakening
- Internal Focus
- Everything good inside initially
- Original Self
- Mindfulness
- I am Whole/Self-Acceptance
- Real Self
- Higher level of Consciousness

- Loving self
- Non-Critical/ Affirmative Self
- Soul /Spirit
- Experiences Wholeness
- Body/Mind/Soul/Spirit
- Dreams/Awakens
- Fully Conscious/Aware/Mindful
- Sensing
- Approaching difficult emotions
- Nourishing
- Living by Values
- Examined Attitudes.
- Examined Beliefs
- Gratitude
- Self-Acceptance/Personal Growth/Comparing with past Self
- Accepting/Ease
- Non-attachment
- Creative Self
- Non-reactive/ Proactive self
- Giving
- I am good enough
- Powerful/Responsible/Proactive
- Goals Set in line with values and beliefs
- Growth Mindset
- Growth
- Opportunity
- Awareness
- Win/Win
- Present Focus

- Examined and Empowering Daily Habits
- Success is the quality of the moments of the journey
- Success is enough
- High levels of consciousness with increasing power, influence, integrity, understanding and compassion.

A Mind Map is presented of the Best Possible Self for further clarification of the key concepts in this Chapter and Book.

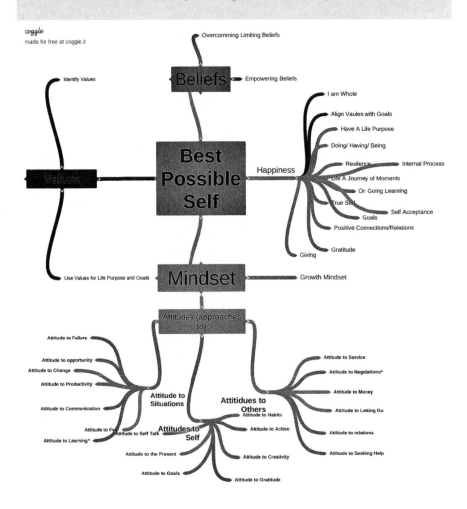

CONCLUSION

Becoming your Best Possible Self, as we have seen in this book, involves a continuous process of self-acceptance, self-improvement and personal growth. This personal growth is based on your Mindset and its three key filters for taking action: Beliefs, Values and Attitudes.

This involves a process of growth which eliminates your limiting beliefs and embraces your empowering beliefs so that you can be true to yourself. The process also requires that you know your values and live your life aligned to these values which in turn will help you to set your Life Purpose.

The final part of the process of growth is to follow a set of attitudes or approaches to yourself, situations and others which will work in tandem with your personal growth and nourish it.

This book has brought you through the process of becoming you Best Possible Self by looking at a new approach to happiness, fulfilment and success.

The old approach is that of doing and having and keep wanting more. This is an outside approach where we search for success outside of ourselves. Our self-esteem is linked with our achievements and possessions. We are constantly comparing with others. We often compete on a win/lose basis. We struggle and strive to get success but it is never enough.

This old approach still dominates. It focuses on externals, it encourages us to aim for personal success, good grades, a good job, monetary success.

The new approach is an inner state of mind. Our self-esteem is based on our mindset and attitude and not our achievement. We open up the mind to the non-physical reality of the world. Success is being true to ourselves and our values. True nobility is not being better than somebody else but being better than you yourself used to be. It is all about growing as a person.

The Waterford doctor Dr Mark Rowe (2015) in his book "A Prescription for Happiness", explains this new approach thus:

"What's most important is not who you were, or even are right now, but who you are becoming along this journey called life."

With this new approach success is motivated by giving and opening to others. Success is often based on win/win thinking. Success encourages ease, relaxation and non-attachment. Success is enough using this approach.

Success is something you attract by the person you become, by your own personal development and what you become is much more important that what you do or have.

This new second approach is the best approach to adopt in my opinion. It is an Inner approach.

In this book this approach is explored using a Model for Taking Action outlined in Chapter 1.

This Model for Taking Action and decisions is described in detail in this book by taking a look into our Mindset which is composed of our three key internal filters: our Beliefs, our Values and our key Attitudes. Positive Psychology is now giving us empirical evidence of the importance of Mindset and its key components for becoming our Best Possible Self.

We saw in Chapter 2 that our Beliefs are very powerful and should be examined to ensure they are serving us or hindering us.

Common limiting beliefs were explored and can seriously hold us back. However as we saw these limiting beliefs can be overcome and challenged using the powerful techniques such as turnaround statements and using empowering beliefs that serve us. One of the most powerful beliefs is our unconditional Self Acceptance and being true to ourselves. Other empowering beliefs were identified and explored such as I am Good enough, I am in Control, I do not need the approval of others and believing in the power of different Attitudes.

In Chapter 3 we explored the second key filter of our Mindset; our Values. Values are defined as our most important things in our lives. However we saw very few people explore their values or know them. This is a big barrier to becoming our Best Possible Self. To be truly happy and fulfilled in our Life we must live our lives in alignment with our values. If we do not know our values how can we do this?

A method for exploring our values was given in chapter 3 and these identified values can also be used for generating our Life Purpose and who we want to Be. It is very important to have a clear vision of who you want to BE. You need to write down the ideal person you want to be. And be crystal clear WHY you want to become this Best Possible Self.

In chapter 4 we looked at the importance of a Growth Mindset which is open to growth and is changeable. The importance of Attitudes which was the third key filter in the Model for Action, is introduced and is defined.

Attitude is our approaches to ourselves, our different situations and our approach to others that best serves us and others.

Three chapters were given over to our key attitudes or approach to ourselves, our situations and others. These attitudes are key approaches or principles which help us on the journey to our Best Possible Self.

In Chapter 5 we explored the first set of key attitudes or approaches to ourselves. In particular we saw we need to listen to the voice in our head, our self-talk, and ask is it supporting us or hindering us. Our relationship with this voice is critical. Negative self-talk is most common (ANTS) but they can be overcome using all the methods shown in this chapter. We also saw that a positive attitude to the here and now (Present) can be transformative and many techniques of staying more present were explored. Positive Attitude to Goals, Gratitude, Creativity, Action and Habits were also explored and contribute significantly to becoming our Best Possible Self by following the advice, examples and exercised given in this chapter.

In Chapter 6 we explored the second set of key attitudes or approaches which we take to different situations in our lives. In particular we saw our attitude or approach to the inevitable failures and adversity in our lives can be critical and can be seen as a significant opportunity for growth and learning. We also saw that other positive attitudes to situations can move us towards becoming our Best Possible Self such as seizing opportunities and welcoming and anticipating change. Other attitudes to situations which were discussed include being productive and not just busy and being attentive to effective communication in particular non verbal cues. We also looked at our attitude to fear which can hold us back but can be overcome. Our attitude to Learning new things outside our comfort zone allows us maximum opportunity to grow as a person. All of these attitudes to situations can contribute to us becoming our Best Possible Self by preparing us to able to have a constructive approach to these common life situations.

In Chapter 7 we explored the third set of key attitudes or approaches we take to other people in our lives. In particular we saw how our attitude to service or serving is key to a fulfilling life and becoming our Best Possible Self. Our attitude to negotiations was seen as optimal where win/win negotiation are possible in most of our dealing with others. An attitude which seeks to let go of emotions and things can be very liberating and we saw forgiveness is hugely beneficial to ourselves. An attitude to Money was given in this chapter which may be a little different from standard advice as it includes contributing to others. We saw that human connection is vital to our happiness and is a core human need and that the quality of our relationships is most important. Finally we have seen that seeking help is a sign of power and is available to us all in many forms. All of these attitudes to others can contribute to becoming our Best Possible Self whilst also contributing positively to others.

In Chapter 8 we revisited the transition from Old Self to Best Possible Self and the key characteristics of each self. The detailed transition table is presented again from the first chapter which after reading the book should be much clearer to you at this stage. The Best Possible Self traits are referenced in the table for easy referral to the specific section in the book where it was explained.

Finally a Mind Map is also presented of the Best Possible Self and some of the key ideas of the book are shown in the map for further clarity.

This book has been an exploration of the new internal approach to becoming our Best Possible Self by looking at the concepts of mindset, beliefs, values and key attitudes for success and happiness. These are based on scientific evidence, studies and my own personal experience and these were referenced throughout the book and are all available to follow further in the Bibliography at the back of this book.

The transition from the External Approach (Old Self) to the Internal Approach (Being the Best Possible Self) is the theme of this book. To not consider this transition is to miss out on what you could have been. In the words of Tony Robbins

"Hell on earth is to meet the man you could have been."

I urge you to consider all the material and advice presented in this book in order for you to become your Best Possibles Self. This is a continuous process of self-improvement self-acceptance and growth which is ongoing. I would encourage you to follow the practical exercises and examples presented in this book in the many "examples" and "try this" sections to reinforce your learning and understanding and help you on your own personal growth journey.

It is said that the key to happiness and success is your power, your wealth, your health and love. These are important, but none of them on their own will bring you true happiness or fulfilment.

The two things, in my opinion, that brings fulfilment and true happiness are… Growth and Service.

Happiness comes from personal progress and growth. From setting value-based goals and working to achieve them. From being true to yourself, serving others and having the right set of beliefs and attitudes – and growing and becoming your Best Possible Self in the process.

That is the key to a joyous, fulfilling, and meaningful life.

Enjoy the Journey!

BIBLIOGRAPHY

Barr, Joe (2021) *Going The Distance* Gill Books

Barry, Harry (2018), *Emotional Resilience*, Orion Publishing Group Ltd.

Beecham Stan (2017) *Elite Minds* Mc Graw Hill Education

Bonnie, Ware (2019) *The 5 Regrets of the Dying* Hay House Inc.

Burg Bob and Mann John, (2015) *The Go Giver* Penguin Books

Canfield, Jack (2006) *The Success Principles*, William Morrow Paperbacks

Canfield, Jack, Hansen, Mark (1993) *Chicken Soup for the Soul*, Vermillion, London

Carrilo Alba et al 2010 *Effects of Best Possible Self Intervention: A systematic review and meta-analysi*s published in PLOS ONE plos.org

Carroll, Ryder, (2021) *The Bullet Journal Method* Forte Estate

Clear James (2018) *Atomic Habits* Penguin Publishing Group

Coelho, Paulo (2020) *The Alchemist 25th Ed.* Harper

Covey Stephen (1989) *7 Habits of Highly Effective People* Simon and Schuster

Dalio Ray (2017) *Principles* Simon and Schuster

David R Hawkins (1995) *Power Versus Force*, Veritas

De Bono Edward (2010) *Lateral Thinking* Harper Collins

Dokhampa, Gualwa (2013) *The Restful Mind*, Yellow Kite, London

Dweck Carol S (2017) *Mindset,* Robinson

Enright, Robert (2015) *8 Key to Forgiveness* WW Norton Company

Frankl, Viktor (2004), *Man's Search for Meaning,* Rider London

Gaffney, Maureen (2021), *Flourishing,* Penguin Books, UK

Gladwell, Malcam, (2008) *Outliers* Penguin

Goleman, Daniel (1995) *Emotional Intelligence,* Bloomsbury London

Grieger, R (2013) *Unconditional Self acceptance, be impeccable with yourself* Psychology Today

Gulliver A et al (2010) " *Perceived barriers and facilitators to mental health help seeking in young people a systematic review*" BMC Psychiatry

Hawkins, David (1995) *Power Vs Force* Hay House

Hay Louise (1984) *You Can Heal Your Life* Hay House

Holden Robert (2011) *Happiness Now* Hay House

Holiday Ryan (2018) *The Obstacle is the Way* Profile Books Ltd.

Holiday Ryan (2016) *The Daily Stoic* Profile Books Ltd.

Hussey, Gerry (2021) *Awaken the Power Within,* Hachette Books Ireland

Jackson, Adam, (1998), *10 Secrets of Abundant Happiness* Thorsons

James Oliver (2007), *Affluenza* Ebury Press

Millburn, Joshua and Nicodemus, Ryan (2011) *Minimalists* Asymmetrical Press

Murphy, Eddie (2015), *Becoming Your Real Self,* Penguin Books, UK

Persaud, Raj (2005), *The Motivated Mind*, Transworld Publishers, London

Ravikart, Kamel (2021) *Love Yourself Like Your Life Depends on It* Harper Collins

Renshaw Ben (2010) *Successful but Something Missing* Ebury Digital

Robbins, Anthony (1992) *Awaken the Giant Within*, Fireside Books, London

Robbins, Mel (2017) *The Five Second Rule* Post Hill Press

Robinson, Ken, *Out of our Minds (2017) The Power of Being Creative*, John Wiley and Sons Ltd.

Rohn Jim (2013) *The Keys to Success* Brolga Publishing

Rowe, Mark (2015), *A Prescription for Happiness*, Kazoo Publishing Services, Dublin

Seligman, Martin (2011) *Flourish*, Nicholas Brealey Publishing, London

Sharma, Robin (1997), *The Monk Who Sold his Ferrari*, Harper Collins Publishers , London

Sharma, Robin (2004), *Discover your Destiny with the Monk who sold his Ferrari*, Harper Thornsons London

Smith, Will (2021) *Will* Penguin UK

Spenser and Johnstown (1998) *Who Moved My Cheese* G.P Putans and Sons

Tolle, Eckhart (2005) *A New Earth* , Penguin Books

Tolle, Eckhart (2005) *The Power of Now*, Penguin Books

Tracey Brian (1993) *Maximum Achievement* Simon Schuster

Turner Colin *(1994) Born to Succeed,* Element Books

Ware, Bonnie (2019) *The Top 5 Regrets of the Dying* Hay House

Warren, Rick (2014) *The Purpose Driven Life* Running Press

Whelan, Dermot (2021) *Mind Full,* Gill Books

Williams, Mark, Penman, Danny (2011) *Mindfulness,* Piatkus London

Young, Webb (2003) *A Technique For Producing Ideas* Mc Graw Hill Education

APPENDIX 1

How to Meditate

Prerequisites before Meditating

- Use a Quiet room
- Have no distractions so no phone/computers/radio on etc
- Sit up with your back straight
- Close your eyes
- If you cannot find time to do it then make time by getting up 10 minutes earlier
- Make note of your start time so that you know how long you were mediating. Often you will be surprised by how fast the time goes and this is a good sign.

Things to notice when meditating using any of the methods

- If thoughts arise when meditating consider this as normal. This is not surprising as we have as many as 80000 thoughts per day.
- Thoughts however can be distracting and often snowball to many other thoughts. If this happens during meditation try to observe or be aware of the thoughts and acknowledge it and if possible, resume you meditation process. Some people find it helpful to label the thought and let it go. i.e., that thought is about my to-do list, what I will make for dinner etc. Give these thoughts no importance and let them go if you can and they will move on.
- Not all meditation styles are right for everyone. These practices require different skills and mindsets. How do you know which

practice is right for you? It's what feels comfortable and what you feel encourages you to practice?

Meditation Methods

Simple Breathing Meditation

1. Ensure all prerequisites (see above)
2. Inhale on the count of 4 and hold for count of 4
3. Exhale on the count of 4 and pause for count of 4
4. Repeat steps 2 – 3 for 4 times

Body Scan Meditation

1. Ensure all prerequisites (see above)
2. Sitting on a chair first focus on your feet and the pressure and sensation of your feet on the ground for a few seconds
3. Then move your attention to the calf muscles for a few seconds notice any feelings or tensions there.
4. Next move your attention to the thigh muscles for a few seconds notice any feelings or tensions there.
5. Next move your attention to the backside area and the pressure on the chair for a few seconds notice any feelings or tensions there.
6. Next move your attention to the stomach area and breathe in on the count of 4 and out on the count of 4. Notice how the stomach muscles contract on the inhale and relax on the exhale.
7. Next move your attention to the shoulder area for a few seconds notice any feelings or tensions there. Shrug your shoulders a few times to release any tension there.
8. Next move your attention to the left upper arm muscles for a few seconds notice any feelings or tensions there.
9. Next move your attention to the left lower arm muscles for a few seconds notice any feelings or tensions there.

10. Next move your attention to the left hand for a few seconds notice any feelings or tensions there. Wiggle all your left-hand fingers.

11. Next move your attention to the right upper arm muscles for a few seconds notice any feelings or tensions there.

12. Next move your attention to the right lower arm muscles for a few seconds notice any feelings or tensions there.

13. Next move your attention to the right hand for a few seconds notice any feelings or tensions there. Wiggle all your right-hand fingers.

14. Next move your attention to the neck muscles for a few seconds notice any feelings or tensions there.

15. Next move your attention to the mouth for a few seconds notice any tastes or sensations there.

16. Next move your attention to the nose for a few seconds there. Inhale on the count of 4 through the nose and hold for a count of 4 and exhale from the nose on a count of 4.

17. Next move your attention to the eyes for a few seconds notice any feelings or tensions there. Move the eyes up and then down 3 times without opening the eyes.

18. Next move your attention to the forehead for a few seconds notice any feelings or tensions there.

19. Next move your attention to the top of the head for a few seconds notice any feelings or tensions there. Move the head to the left and to the right 3 times.

20. Finally move you attention to your hearing. Focus on the sounds around you, ticking clock, car on the street moving, bird sound, voices, follow the sounds and notice if they are moving towards or away from you. Do this listening for a few minutes, if possible, with the aim to extend the listening period over time.

Mantra Meditation

1. Ensure all Prerequisites
2. Focus on repeating a word over and over again slowly for a few minutes.
3. Normally the word to repeat has no meaning to the person so you are not thinking about the meaning of the word only how the sound of the word resonates. For example, words with many vowels are used such as " MAR-AN-A-TA."

My Preferred Meditation Method

I like to combine the three meditation methods above together Body Scan, Breathing and Mantra Meditations.

When I finish the extended Body scan, and Breathing Meditation I will then practice the Mantra Meditation using the word "MARANATA" for a minimum of 10 minutes. The entire meditation usually takes approximately 17 minutes.

The Meditation I practice daily has 3 components done one after the other.

1. The Body Scan Meditation (5 minutes)
2. Simple Breathing Meditation (2 minutes)
3. Mantra Meditation (10 minutes)

APPENDIX 2

Best Possible Self Exercise

What is a Best Possible Self Exercise

The Best Possible Self Exercise consists of a short writing exercise in which you imagine your Best Possible Self in a potential future <u>when a lot has gone well</u>. Multiple studies by Carrillo Alba et al 2010 have shown it is a very beneficial exercise.

The researchers conducted a meta analysis of many studies which were selected because they required a written best-possible-self exercise to be carried out. The result was that participants displayed more optimism and hope following the completion of the exercise compared to those who did not do the exercise.

Instructions

1. Over a one week period spend at least 30 minutes per day filling in all the questions A. to E. below.

2. Imagine yourself in a future where things have gone well.. Do not over exaggerate your greatest goal achievements, but set goals that are achievable in the real world.

3. The timeline given below is in 2 years, but you could change the timeline yourself to 6 months, 1 year or 10 years.

A. <u>Values</u>

List your <u>current</u> Values to ensure your goals achieved in B. below are aligned with your current Values (see Chapter 3 for how to discover your Values).

1.

2.

3.

4.

5.

6.

7.

8.

<u>B.Goals Achieved</u>

List key goals achieved in key areas of your life in 2 years time assuming everything is going well (ie the best case scenario). Make sure that these goals achieved are aligned to your key values listed in A.above where possible.

Family Goals Achieved

Key Relationship Goals Achieved

Career Goals Achieved

Hobbiies/Interests Goals Achieved

Health Goals Achieved

Friends Goals Achieved

Personal Project Goals Achieved

C.What type of person do I wish to BE

List the traits that you want to have and BE in two years time. Again assuming everything is going well (see section 3.2 in Chapter 3)

1.

2.

3.

4.

5.

6.

7.

8.

D.Key Attitudes

List Key Attitudes you will have and will use in 2 years time (see sections 5.8, 6.8 and 7.7 for a summary of the key attitudes to self, situations and others) again assuming all is going well.

E. Key Beliefs

List Key Empowering Beliefs you will have and will use in 2 years time. (see section 2.4) again assuming all is going well.

INDEX

A

Acceptance, 6,7,8,10,34,35,
36,50,52,53,54,55,59,218,
221,222
Achievable, 104,110,111,112,239
Actions, 15,17,18,20,22,23,
32,34,41,42,50,
64,77,128,171,206,216,217
Addiction, 5,28,95,211
Adversity, 11,44,68,135,140,
143,145,146,147,148,179,
215,217,220,222,228
Affirmations,
74,75,76,84,86,136,160,172
Anxiety,
5,95,170,173,196,199,211
Appreciation,
6,51,52,53,98,115,216
Assessment, 40,45
Attitudes, 4,5,9,11,12,15,16,
17,22,23,34,43,
44,46,47,62,63,64,65,66,67,
68,69,70,121,135,136,138,
139,158,159,179,181,213,
216,217,219,221,223,225,
226,227,228,229,230
Attitudes to Others, 44,67,
68,181,213,229
Attitudes to Self, 43,47,67,
69,70,136
Attitudes to Situations,44,
68,139,179,228

B

Balance, 38,41,51,52,53,58,
66,126
Behaviour, 16,19,22,25,26,
48,79,80,146,157,168,206
Being the Best, 51,216,229
Beliefs, 4,5,9,11,15,16,17,18,
20,22,23,24,25,26,27,28,29,
31,32,33,34,43,45,46,47,63,
64,65,67,68,69,70,86,104,105,
109,138,143,158,159,173,179,
196,215,216,217,219,220,221,
223,225,226,227,229,230
Bias, 8,73,74,85,117,125,126,
127,134,137,153
Brainstorming, 123,160

C

Capacity, 24,36,154
Change, 11,30,33,43,44,48,
49,54,62,63,64,65,68,73,79,
81,82,84,104,107,108,127,
130,135,138,143,144,145,154,
155,156,157,176,179,215,217,
220,228,239,247
Cheerfulness, 51,52,53
Commitment, 51,53,54,59,
109,186
Common Limiting Beliefs,
25,27,45,46,226
Communication, 44,68,138,

162,164,165,166,167,177,17
9,180,190,201,228
Compassion,
36,43,51,52,53,79,82,224
Consciousness,
10,11,34,35,36,37,47,90,96,
203,218,221,222,224
Creativity, 4,33,37,44,51,53,
67,70,90,120,121,122,134,
136,137,144,177,196,
217,228

D

Dedication, 51,53
Determination, 33,144
Difficulty, 27,72,120,138,140,
141,142,145,146,151

E

Ego, 6,8,10,27,28,35,38,46,
58,87,215,219,221
Empathy,
51,53,62,165,199,248
Empowering Beliefs,
25,33,34,43,45,47,225,
227,244
Encouragement, 51,52,53
Enthusiasm, 51,53,186
Ethics, 51,104

F

Failure, 44,59,63,68,111,

128,138,140,141,142,145,
146,149,154,176,179
Fear, 27,36,38,44,59,68,72,83,
89,107,111,
115,128,130,135,138,142,
170,171,172,173,174,176,
180,215,228,247
Fearful self, 10,218,221
Flexibility, 51,52,53,160
Forgiveness,134,195,196,
199,213,228,232

G

Generosity, 51,193
Goals, 11,31,41,43,60,67,
70,74,75,101,102,103,104,
105,106,107,108,109,110,
111,112,113,114,128,134,
135,136,151,152,158,160,
191,215,217,220,222,223,
228,230,239,240,241,
241,242
Gratitude, 11,44,63,67,70,
85,115,116,117,118,134,
136,187,216,217,218,219,
223,228

H

Habits, 11,41,44,48,67,70,
99,102,130,131,132,133,
135,137,182,188,196,220,
222,224,228,231
Humility, 38,51,53

I

Importance of attitude, 4,65,66
Independence, 51,52,53,112
Inferiority Complex, 38
Inner voice, 56,71,74,80,136
Innovation, 51,123,126
Inspirations,25,38,43,46, 58,121,135,216,217
Integrity, 36,189,224

K

Key Attitudes, 5,9,43,44, 63,66,67,68,69,70, 136,138,139,179,181,213, 216,217,226,227,228, 229,243
Key influences, 15,22
Kindness, 51,52,53,58,95,184,187
Kinesiology, 36

L

Law of Attraction, 79,84,85, 86,112
Leadership, 3,51,53,159,185
Learning, 2,3,4,5,13,16,44,51, 53,68,82,122,134,138,146, 148,149,175,176,177,178,179, 180,210,216,217,228,230
Let go, 48,83,147,155,195, 196,198,199,200,228
Life Purpose,5,49,56,57,58,59, 60,61,134,135,158,159,179, 225,227
Loving self, 10,218,223

M

Meditation, 90,93,94,95,96,97,100, 120,134, 136,172,235,236,238
Mentorship, 209,210,213
Mindfulness, 10,51,52,53, 90,93,95,97,98,99,100,134,136, 197,218,222,234
Mindsets, 12,62,63,64,236
Model for Action, 15,16, 19,21,23,25,49,63,227

N

Natural, 2,27,31,41,116,128, 154,168,171,172,180,197
Negative thinking, 73,78,81,83
Negotiations, 44,69,181,188, 189,190,213,228
Nourishing, 10,219,223

O

Old Self, 9,10,12,14,214, 215,216,218,221,229
Opportunity, 11,44,64,68, 73,77,99,100,117,138,140, 142,143,146,150,151,152, 174,179,189,220,223,228
Optimism, 51,52,53,55,79,

80,115,239
Overcoming Limiting
Beliefs, 25,32

P

Passions, 25,38,39,40,
43,46,56,57,58,60,
105,106,121,135,198,216,
217
Peace, 35,36,51,52,53,88,
97,171,195,196
Perfection, 9,27,51,128
Personal growth, 11,13,14,
111,196,199,219,223,
225,230
Perspectives,12,33,122,
144,151,177,199
Positive self-talk,20,63,71,
72,74,84,136
Proactive, 11,41,42,51,53,
55,126,133,219,220,223
Productivity,44,68,138,
158,159,160,179,190
Progress, 41,104,111,112,
118,126,140,146,217,230

R

Real Self, 10,29,218,222,232
Relationships, 44,52,53,69,
106,120,126,135,181,186,189,
196,198,201,202,203,204,205,
213,216,218,229
Relish, 93,100,136
Resilience, 4,35,52,53,145,

156,199
Responsibility, 30,32,41,52

S

Self-acceptance, 6,11,13,14,
35,37,40,46,72,75,216,219,22
2,223,225,229
Self-awareness, 37,40,95
Self-esteem, 7,27,74,215,
216,225
Self-improvement, 13,130,
225,229
Self-knowledge, 37,43
Self-talk, 18,20,43,63,67,70,71,
72,73,74,79,80,81,82,84,86,
136,215,227,228
Spirituality, 52,53,106
Subconscious, 75,76,89,
120,151

T

Thoughtfulness, 52,53
Time Management,
121,158,159
True self, 37,38,39,40,46,
47,59,90,217,218

U

Understanding, 3,5,13,34,36,
52,166,169,177,196,224,
230,248
Unhappiness, 5,7,49,89

V

Values, 4,5,7,9,11,12,15,16,17,
22,23,34,40,43,46,48,49,50,
52,54,55,56,57,59,60,61,63,
64,65,67,68,69,70,103,104,
108,109,121,135,138,158,
159,160,179,181,216,217,
219,220,221,223,225,226,
227,229,240
Vision,9,52,58,107,108,112,
227,247

W

Well-Being, 12,52,53,199
Wisdom, 4,52,107

PLEASE REVIEW

If you enjoyed this book, I would really appreciate if you could spread the word and if you purchased this book from an online bookstore, please do leave a review. Your opinion counts and it does influence buyer decision on whether to purchase the book or not and in turn this will contribute to a very worthy charity, where 100% of the profits from the sale of this book will be donated to Samaritans Ireland, registered charity 20033668. Please mail me on becomingyourbestpossibleself@gmail.com for feedback or any queries. Thank you.

BONUS ITEMS

Please email becomingyourbestpossibleself@gmail.com for the following bonus resources.

A downloadable workbook for Appendix 2 for you to answer the questions and record your observations.

A bonus mini ebook with key takeaways from the book.

ABOUT THE SAMARITANS

Samaritans Ireland is a registered charity (20033668) dedicated to providing emotional support and preventing suicide. Operating in Ireland and Northern Ireland, Samaritans offers a vital service that aims to help individuals who are in distress, feeling overwhelmed, or contemplating self-harm or suicide.

- Samaritans' vision is that fewer people die by suicide.
- Samaritans' mission is to make sure there's someone there for anyone who needs someone.

The primary service Samaritans provides is a confidential telephone helpline, 116 123, that is available 24 hours a day, 365 days a year. Anyone who is struggling emotionally, experiencing loneliness, or going through a difficult time can reach out to Samaritans for a listening ear. The helpline is staffed by 2,000 trained volunteers in 21 branches in Ireland and Northern Ireland who provide a safe space for individuals to express their feelings and thoughts without fear of criticism or rejection.

In addition to its direct support services, Samaritans works to raise awareness of the issues surrounding suicide and self-harm. The organisation engages in public education campaigns to promote mental health awareness, reduce stigma surrounding mental health issues, and encourage individuals to seek help if they are struggling.

Samaritans Ireland also works with other organisations and stakeholders in the mental health space to develop comprehensive and integrated support services for individuals in need. The organisation recognises that addressing the issue of suicide and self-harm requires a multi-faceted and collaborative approach, and it works to build partnerships and coalitions to promote positive change in Ireland's mental health landscape.

Samaritans' approach to addressing the incidence of suicide and self-harm in Ireland is rooted in empathy, support, and collaboration. Through their work they seek to create a culture of openness and understanding around mental health issues, and to provide comprehensive and effective support services to individuals who may be struggling with their mental health.

Colm Dolan
Head of Income Generation
Samaritans Ireland

https://www.samaritans.org/ireland/samaritans-ireland/
Samaritans Ireland is a charity registered in the Republic of Ireland (20033668) and incorporated in the Republic of Ireland as a company limited by guarantee (450409).

Printed in Great Britain
by Amazon

43865667R00145